DATE DUE	

THE CELTS

Other titles in the *Lost Civilizations* series include:

The Ancient Greeks
The Ancient Romans
Empires of Mesopotamia
The Mayans
The Vikings

LOST CIVILIZATIONS

THE CELTS

Allison Lassieur

LUCENT BOOKS
P.O. BOX 289011
SAN DIEGO, CA 92198-9011

Library of Congress Cataloging-in-Publication Data

Lassieur, Allison
    The Celts / by Allison Lassieur.
        p. cm. — (Lost civilizations series)
    ISBN 1-56006-756-X (alk. paper)
    1. Celts—Juvenile literature. 2. Civilization, Celtic—Juvenile literature [1. Celts.
2. Civilization, Celtic.] I. Title. II Lost civilizations (San Diego, Calif.)
    D70 .L32 2001
909'.04916—dc21

                                                                        00-011302

Copyright © 2001 by Lucent Books, Inc.
P.O. Box 289011, San Diego, CA 92198-9011
Printed in the U.S.A.

CONTENTS

FOREWORD

"What marvel is this?" asked the noted eighteenth-century German poet and philosopher, Friedrich Schiller. "O earth . . . what is your lap sending forth? Is there life in the deeps as well? A race yet unknown hiding under the lava?" The "marvel" that excited Schiller was the discovery, in the early 1700s, of two entire ancient Roman cities buried beneath over sixty feet of hardened volcanic ash and lava near the modern city of Naples, on Italy's western coast. "Ancient Pompeii is found again!" Schiller joyfully exclaimed. "And the city of Hercules rises!"

People had known about the existence of long lost civilizations before Schiller's day, of course. Stonehenge, a circle of huge, very ancient stones had stood, silent and mysterious, on a plain in Britain as long as people could remember. And the ruins of temples and other structures erected by the ancient inhabitants of Egypt, Palestine, Greece, and Rome had for untold centuries sprawled in magnificent profusion throughout the Mediterranean world. But when, why, and how were these monuments built? And what were the exact histories and beliefs of the peoples who built them? A few scattered surviving ancient literary texts had provided some partial answers to some of these questions. But not until Pompeii and Herculaneum started to emerge from the ashes did the modern world begin to study and re-

construct lost civilizations in a systematic manner.

Even then, the process was at first slow and uncertain. Pompeii, a bustling, prosperous town of some twenty thousand inhabitants, and the smaller Herculaneum met their doom on August 24, A.D. 79 when the nearby volcano, Mt. Vesuvius, blew its top and literally erased them from the map. For nearly seventeen centuries, their contents, preserved in a massive cocoon of volcanic debris, rested undisturbed. Not until the early eighteenth century did people begin raising statues and other artifacts from the buried cities; and at first this was done in a haphazard, unscientific manner. The diggers, who were seeking art treasures to adorn their gardens and mansions, gave no thought to the historical value of the finds. The sad fact was that at the time no trained experts existed to dig up and study lost civilizations in a proper manner.

This unfortunate situation began to change in 1763. In that year, Johann J. Winckelmann, a German librarian fascinated by antiquities (the name then used for ancient artifacts), began to investigate Pompeii and Herculaneum. Although he made some mistakes and drew some wrong conclusions, Winckelmann laid the initial, crucial groundwork for a new science—archaeology (a term derived from two Greek words meaning "to talk about ancient things." His book, *History of the Art of Antiquity*, became a model for the first generation of archaeologists to follow in their efforts to understand other lost civilizations. "With unerring sensitivity," noted scholar C.W. Ceram explains, "Winckelmann groped toward original insights, and expressed them with such power of language that the cultured European world was carried away by a wave of enthusiasm for the antique ideal. This . . . was of prime importance in shaping the course of archaeology in the following century. It demonstrated means of understanding ancient cultures through their artifacts."

In the two centuries that followed, archaeologists, historians, and other scholars began to piece together the remains of lost civilizations around the world. The glory that was Greece, the grandeur that was Rome, the cradles of human civilization in Egypt's Nile valley and Mesopotamia's Tigris-Euphrates valley, the colorful royal court of ancient China's Han Dynasty, the mysterious stone cities of the Maya and Aztecs in Central America—all of these

and many more were revealed in fascinating, often startling, if sometimes incomplete detail by the romantic adventure of archaeological research. This work, which continues, is vital. "Digs are in progress all over the world," says Ceram. "For we need to understand the past five thousand years in order to master the next hundred years."

Each volume in the *Lost Civilizations* series examines the history, works, everyday life, and importance of ancient cultures. The archaeological discoveries and methods used to gather this knowledge are stressed throughout. Where possible, quotes by the ancients themselves, and also by later historians, archaeologists, and other experts support and enliven the text. Primary and secondary sources are carefully documented by footnotes and each volume supplies the reader with an extensive Works Consulted list. These and other research tools, including glossaries and time lines, afford the reader a thorough understanding of how a civilization that was long lost has once more seen the light of day and begun to reveal its secrets to its captivated modern descendants.

THE WORLD OF THE ANCIENT CELTS

Of all the ancient peoples, the Celts most inspire the imagination. Even the word Celt brings to mind a host of images: thatched houses, harps, stone crosses, and windswept coastlines. The Celts' world was filled with bloody warfare, golden treasures, haunting music, magnificent warrior kings, and mysterious druids. They were fighters, boasters, kinsmen, and kings. They worshiped pagan gods. They made beautiful jewelry and artwork.

The Celts emerged from history to become one of the first great civilizations north of the Alps. Some historians have dubbed them "the first Europeans," for this reason. By the third century B.C., the Celts had expanded throughout Europe, north to Ireland, south to Spain, and even into Russia and Ukraine.

The Celts were ferocious fighters, and they left quite an impression on the Greeks and Romans who fought them in battle. They defeated Roman armies and invaded Greece. Some Celtic tribes even established their civilization in what is now Turkey. The Greeks were so impressed with the Celts that they recruited them to fight in their own armies. The Ptolemaic rulers of Egypt used Celtic troops in their Egyptian armies. Later, after the Romans invaded the Celtic areas of

Gaul, Celtic warriors even fought in the enemy Roman armies.

But the Celts were much more than warriors. They were scientists and thinkers. Their society was based on agriculture, and they created advanced farming innovations. Their fields produced enough grain to feed many parts of Europe. They had highly trained physicians and scientists who were respected throughout the classical world. Their magnificent earthen structures, called hill-forts, were masterpieces of architectural ingenuity. Long before the Romans built roadways, the Celts built roads into the deep forests and wildernesses of Europe and Great Britain.

They were also poets and storytellers. During the Christian era, they created some of the richest literature that has been left by any culture. This literature was based on ancient, glorious stories that storytellers had passed down for generations, stories that recount the exploits of gods, goddesses, magic, and heroes.

This vast wealth of knowledge and culture thrived in Europe for hundreds of years. Then, slowly, it was crushed under the weight of invasion and conquest. The great Celtic tribes that roamed and settled Europe were destroyed one by one. By about A.D.

1000, the last remnants of the Celtic civilization had been erased from Europe, and few remembered that the Celts had given the world art, wealth, and culture.

A Skewed Roman View

The Romans had much to do with this. During their invasions of Celtic lands, they wrote many stinging accounts of the barbaric tribes they faced. Although a few ancient writers attempted to give an objective view of the Celts, many others vilified them as wild, uneducated, animal-like children who were better off subdued.

Their words had the effect that they hoped: Romans and others in the so-called civilized world—especially those that the Celts had once defeated—thought of the Celts in the worst light. They believed there was nothing redeeming about the civilization and that it was fine if the Celts were destroyed. The image of the wild-eyed Celt gnashing his teeth in battle is an image created and perpetuated by the Romans, and it is the image that lasted through the centuries.

The Roman Accounts Prove Incorrect

Scholars as recently as the nineteenth century believed that image to be correct. Few archaeologists studied Celtic history because the common belief was that the Roman accounts were accurate. But there were hints that this might not be altogether true. The Celts' grand hill-forts still stood in parts of England and Europe. Rare examples of beautiful jewelry and artwork existed in museums. Occasionally, archaeologists dredged up Celtic artifacts from rivers and lakes, but nothing that suggested concretely that the Celts were any better than their Roman reputations.

Then, two great archaeological discoveries in Europe during the nineteenth century changed all that. One was the discovery of an ancient Iron Age salt mine and cemetery in Hallstatt, Austria. The salt had preserved many Celtic artifacts, which revealed a rich and vibrant Celtic community. The other was a marvelous archaeological find on the shores of Lake Neuchâtel in Switzerland. So many Celtic artifacts were found in an area now known as La Tène, that historians speculate it could have been a major Celtic trading community.

All of this evidence destroyed the long-held idea that the Celts were barbaric and uneducated. The communities at Hallstatt and La Tène showed that the Celts had an advanced society rich in both culture and technology. Other finds, including a Celtic prince's grave in Hochdorf, Germany, in 1978, further prove that the Celtic civilization was much, much more than their Roman enemies had revealed.

CHAPTER ONE

THE FIRST EUROPEANS

The day of July 18, 390 B.C. dawned in Rome just like any other day. Citizens of the grand, ancient city went about their business, unaware that their world was about to come to a crashing end. Just eleven miles outside the city, a huge Roman army had gathered near the river Allia. These professional soldiers were massing to meet a strange, fearsome army: warriors from a wild Celtic tribe called the Senones. The legions of Roman soldiers had no reason to fear these strangers. This rabble of unwashed, rough soldiers could be easily defeated. After all, Rome was used to battling—and defeating—barbarians.

True, some had heard stories of the rough Celts who faced them: they lived somewhere in the north, and they traded goods with the Greeks. There might even have been whispers through the Roman ranks of their fearlessness in battle. But most of the Romans who faced the Celts that day had never seen or heard of them. As historian Peter Berresford Ellis writes:

> [The Romans] viewed [the Celts], perhaps, with some awe, as they watched their opponents' light cavalry position itself; as the terrifying war chariots drew up in lines and the outwardly undisciplined infantry took up their positions. . . . [The Celts] sang boastful war songs, roared battle cries and shouted taunts towards the

. . . ranks of Romans. They were brightly attired, wore patterned trousers, a sight few Romans had seen before, and colorful cloaks. Their leaders wore gold torques [thick rings] around their necks and other rich jewelry. They carried long shields and equally long slashing swords.[1]

There is no written record of what the Celts thought as they gazed upon the polished ranks of the Roman army. But there is no disputing what the Celts did that day. For on that morning, they destroyed the Roman army and marched toward Rome. In the next few days, these strangers from the north would sack the greatest city in the ancient world and shake the foundations of Europe for centuries to come.

To the Romans, the Celts were a nightmare come horribly to life. Their descriptions of the Celtic armies they fought give the impression that the Celts were a terrifying race of animal-like humans bent on blood lust and destruction. It is these ancient descriptions that have shaped modern thinking about the Celtic civilization, and most of these impressions are far from complimentary. As historian David Willis McCullough explains,

> As described by classical Roman historians (who more often than not were

actually Greek), the various tribes of the Celts . . . that streamed out of the north were creatures of boundless, unfocused chaos. They appeared suddenly out of nowhere. They were noisy. They did not fight the way armies were supposed to fight. They slept with everyone: their sisters, their comrades, anyone. They drank something stronger than wine. They had all those horses. They were blond. Some of them even fought naked. And they were big. The barbarians' size is mentioned so often, it is hard not to suspect that the Romans were really quite short and perhaps self-conscious about it.[2]

The Celts were a mystery to almost everyone who came in contact with them. Few knew who they were or how they lived. Many ancient historians, intrigued by this new race of warlike people, wrote about them. It is from these writings that an image of the Celts has emerged.

Known From Writings of Other Cultures

The Celts did not have a written language of their own. As a result, almost nothing is known about their society from their point of view. The majority of the information about the Celtic civilization comes from the writings of other cultures who traded, fought, and lived alongside them for more than 700 years, from about the sixth century B.C. until about the first century A.D.

The earliest mention of the Celts can be found in a Roman coastal survey. That

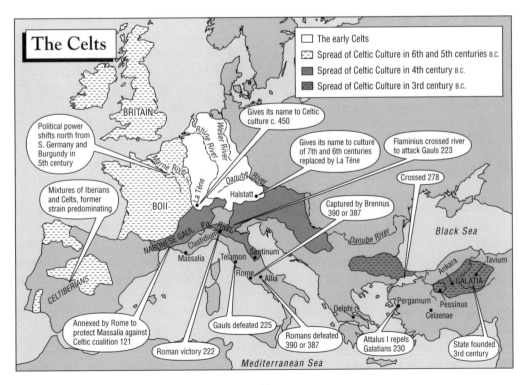

The Celts

- ☐ The early Celts
- ⊟ Spread of Celtic Culture in 6th and 5th centuries B.C.
- ▨ Spread of Celtic Culture in 4th century B.C.
- ▨ Spread of Celtic Culture in 3rd century B.C.

BRITAIN

Political power shifts north from S. Germany and Burgundy in 5th century

Mixtures of Iberians and Celts, former strain predominating

Gives its name to Celtic culture c. 450

Gives its name to culture of 7th and 6th centuries replaced by La Téne

Flaminius crossed river to attack Gauls 223

Crossed 278

Rhine River
Weser River
Marne River
La Téne
Danube River
Halstatt

BOII

NARBONESE GAUL
Po River
Clastidium
Massalia
Telamon
Sentinum
Rome
Allia

Captured by Brennus 390 or 387

Danube River

Black Sea

CELTIBERIANS

Annexed by Rome to protect Massalia against Celtic coalition 121

Roman victory 222

Gauls defeated 225

Romans defeated 390 or 387

Delphi

Pergamum
Celaenae
Pessinus

Ankara
GALATIA
Tavium

Attalus I repels Galatians 230

State founded 3rd century

Mediterranean Sea

11

document, although compiled in about A.D. 566, includes a description of the Mediterranean coast from the early sixth century B.C. It describes the Celts living in specific areas of Europe centuries before they are mentioned in other accounts. The document, according to historian Barry Cunliffe, "gives a clear impression that peoples, who could be classed together as Celts, lived close to the North Sea, in France, and in the southwest of Spain."[3]

Many early surviving documents that mention the Celts, like the coastal survey, usually mention only where the civilization lived in relation to the so-called civilized world of the Greeks and Romans. As historians Myles Dillon and Nora Chadwick explain in their book, *The Celtic Realms,*

> At the end of the sixth century B.C. the Celts were already known to Greek historians and ethnographers. Hecataeus of Miletus [Greek historian], writing at about that time, says that [a city called] Narbonne is a Celtic town, and mentions [another city called] Marseilles as being near Celtic territory. Herodotus [Greek historian], in the fifth century, twice mentions the Celts . . . only to say that the Danube [a river in Germany] has its source . . . amongst the Celts, and that they dwell beyond the [area called] Pillars of Hercules and are the most westerly people in Europe.[4]

Although historians can point to these documents as evidence that the Celts were widespread by this time, little else is known about the specific Celtic societies. It would be up to the Romans to give more details of the Celtic civilization, especially their experiences with the Celts during war.

Roman Descriptions of Celts

The Romans left many descriptions of Celts, especially in warfare. It is from these accounts that information about the Celts has survived. One of the most famous accounts can be found in *The Gallic War,* written by Julius Caesar. This famous Roman commander invaded Gaul (now the area of France and Belgium) in 58 B.C. and fought the Celts, whom he called Gauls, for about seven years. The book is his account of his experiences there. In *The Gallic War,* Caesar gives many descriptions about the customs of the Celts, including this one concerning the Celt attitude toward warfare,

> Their whole life is occupied in hunting and in the pursuits of the military art; from childhood they devote themselves to fatigue and hardships. Those who have remained chaste for the longest time receive the greatest commendation among their people: they think that by this the growth is promoted, by this the physical powers are increased and the sinews are strengthened.[5]

Another writer, Diodorus Siculus, included brief descriptions of Celtic military and society in his massive, forty-book encyclopedia *The Library of History,* written about 50 B.C. He was not nearly as respectful of the Celts as Caesar when he wrote,

> The Gauls are exceedingly addicted to the use of wine and fill themselves with the wine which is brought into

HOW DID THE CELTS GET THEIR NAME?

Around 600 B.C., Greek merchants made a treaty with another group to trade goods for the silver that the group mined in their lands far from Greece. The king of this foreign group was named Arganthonios, and the name of his people, according to the Greek record, was Keltoi.

Keltoi is a Greek word, but it was the name that the Celts called themselves. The Greeks wrote it as they heard it from the native pronunciation. Some historians speculate that the word *Celt* came from the prefix *kel-*, which is a part of the Indo-European language system and means hidden. Other clues come from the Irish, in which the word *celim* means "I hide." The word *celt* can also be seen in the name for a piece of clothing known as a kilt.

The Celts were a private, somewhat mysterious people. They did not believe in recording their knowledge in written form. As a result, some scholars think that it is quite likely that the Celts referred to themselves as the hidden people—the Keltoi.

their country by merchants, drinking it unmixed, and since they partake of this drink without moderation by reason of their craving for it, when they are drunken they fall into a stupor or a state of madness.[6]

Regardless of the disdain with which some people viewed the Celts, their contemporaries considered them to be one of the most powerful groups in Europe. These writers spoke of the Celts as *barbarians*, which only meant that they spoke a different language. (The Greeks and Romans called anyone who didn't speak their language barbarians.) Many ancient writers mention the strength of the Celtic barbarians that lived beyond the borders of the civilized world of the Greeks and Romans.

As historian T. G. E. Powell comments, "The Greeks recognized the Celts to be a major barbarian people living west and north of the Western Mediterranean, and beyond the Alps. Ephorus [an ancient historian], writing in the fourth century B.C., counted the Celts amongst the four great barbarian peoples of the known world."[7]

No information exists as to how the Celts became such a powerful group. The evidence scientists have found is sketchy at best, giving tantalizing hints about the culture rather than absolute truths. The only sources that have survived are archaeological evidence, fragments of the Celtic oral culture in the form of myths and stories, and the writings of the people who came in contact with them. From these sources, a picture of the Celtic civilization has slowly emerged.

Origins of the Celtic Civilization

The earliest Celts probably descended from a group that archaeologists refer to as the Urnfield culture, which is usually dated to about 1200 B.C. No one knows what these people called themselves, but archaeologists coined the term *Urnfield* because the culture cremated their dead and put the remains in urns, which they buried together in cemeteries. The Urnfield culture rose in the very heart of Europe—what is now Germany, France, and Switzerland. As Peter Berresford Ellis explains,

> In the . . . Urnfield culture we see the early beginnings of what we now call the Celtic civilization. This civilization, as we would recognize it, emerged in what is now eastern France, north Alpine Switzerland and south-west Germany, at the headwaters of the Danube, the Rhine and the Rhone [Rivers].[8]

So little evidence remains of the Urnfield culture that archaeologists can only guess at what it was like. But the few material remains that have been found suggest this group was almost certainly the ancestor of the Celts. Evidence of timber fortifications at an Urnfield village site in Wittnaur Horn in Switzerland show that the culture was powerful enough to conduct warfare and cohesive enough to plan and build large structures, such as the later Celts were able to do. The village held about seventy houses, which suggests that about three hundred people lived there. From this, historians speculate that the town, because of its substantial size, must have had a working social structure such as some kind of government or central leader.

Likewise, although the burials were cremations, the Urnfields did include some grave goods with the remains. Two of these burials, which date to about the twelfth century B.C., show close links to the Celtic culture that was to come. The strongest evidence is the appearance of horse trappings in the grave goods. The Celts were among the first people to use horses, so these artifacts suggest a strong link between the two cultures. Other objects, such as decorated weapons, were similar to later Celtic finds. Nora Chadwick describes these:

> One grave contained a number of items of bronze horse-gear—cheek pieces, bits, harness mounts and the like—implying that the dead man was sufficiently prestigious to have owned a horse. In another grave . . . the cremation was accompanied by a number of ancillary pots, three bronze vessels, a sword and knife and a gold spiral ornament. More surprising was the fact that a wagon, represented by its bronze fittings, had been involved in funerary rituals.[9]

Early Language Influences

Another link between the Urnfield and Celtic civilizations can be found in the place-names throughout Europe, especially in the areas of Switzerland, Germany, and France. Many areas in which traces of the Urnfield culture have been found also have Celtic place-names. For example, the names of the three European rivers where Urnfield artifacts have been found—the Danube, the Rhine, and the Rhone—all come from the Celtic language. *Danube* comes from Danu, the Celtic Mother Goddess. The name *Rhine* comes from an an-

A Cinerary Urn used by the Urnfield culture. The Urnfields cremated their dead and kept the ashes inside urns like the one pictured above.

cient Celtic word for the sea. The name *Rhone*, once known as *Rhodanus*, also comes from the word *Danu*. This link enables scholars to point to specific areas of Europe where the early Celts probably lived. Ellis explains that, "With the emergence of the Urnfield culture of Central Europe, there appeared a people whom some scholars regard as being 'proto-Celtic,' in that they may have spoken, as is suggested by place-names, an early form of Celtic."[10]

Centuries later, when the Celts migrated throughout Europe and Great Britain, they continued to give places unique names. Historians and archaeologists can follow the trail to trace the history and movements of the Celtic culture. For example, place-names such as the Avon River, the city of London, and the county of Kent in England came from the early Celts.

The Urnfield culture lived in this area for centuries, but little more is known about their culture. Slowly, other groups migrated to the areas around the Urnfield, bringing with them their own culture and language. Around the world, especially in the Mediterranean and in Asia Minor, warfare and migration meant that people were flooding into the area once inhabited only by the early Urnfield.

These immigrants brought new languages into areas where people had once spoken only the early Celtic tongues. As a result, the culture that was to become the Celtic civilization had a very different language from its neighbors. Eventually, this difference in language became a distinguishing mark that separated the Celtic civilization from the rest of the world. Ellis details this in his book *Celt and Roman,*

> From their earliest appearance in written records, they [the Celts] are clearly identified by the fact that they spoke languages which can be distinguished from other European languages by the term 'Celtic' . . . the Celtic languages spread rapidly during the first millennium B.C. as the Celtic tribes . . . were able to construct roads through the previously impenetrable forests of Northern Europe.[11]

The Hallstatt Culture

The Urnfield culture gave way to the next development in the Celtic history, known as the Hallstatt culture. Archaeologists point to the Hallstatt culture as the first true, developed Celtic civilization in Europe. This period lasted roughly from 1000–500 B.C. and was a time when the Celts rose to prominence among the Europeans.

The name *Hallstatt* comes from the name of a small, isolated area in Austria where, during the 1800s, archaeologists unearthed a magnificent Celtic cemetery. Hundreds of graves have been excavated, shedding light on the power of the early Celtic civilization.

A major hallmark of the Celtic people of the Hallstatt period is their superior iron weapons and tools. The Celts possessed thousands of beautiful objects, many of which they buried with their dead. According to one writer,

> vessels, weapons of iron, personal decorations such as buckles, armlets, rings and neck ornaments were recovered, many of them bearing symbols familiar to later Celtic iconography, such as the ram-headed serpent and the cross in various forms, symbolic of the sun. Buckets and . . . actual joints of meat, especially pig-meat, were excavated in these graves, and all these objects testify to the prosperity of the society, its innovating nature, and its new and exciting style.[12]

The most distinctive objects archaeologists unearthed were beautiful wagons. In many burials, Hallstatt Celts laid the body of their leader on or under a large, four-wheeled wagon. This wagon, along with other rich grave goods, was then buried in a large earthen mound. The existence of these wagons suggests that the Celts had developed advanced transportation technology long before anyone else in Europe. As Ellis indicates, "A feature of these burials of 'chieftains' [leaders] was that the bodies were laid out on four-wheeled wagons with splendidly decorative yokes and harnesses. The sophistication of the wagons and their means of construction indicate that the Celts had become highly advanced in methods of transport."[13]

Celts Establish Flourishing Trade

Many of the objects found at Hallstatt were made by the Celts themselves, but others were clearly the work of outside cultures.

A major hallmark of the Celts during the Hallstatt period was their superior weapons and tools.

This indicates that the Celts had established trade with many other cultures throughout Europe, and the goods they traded were of the highest quality. Historian Anne Ross describes the profusion of imported goods found at Hallstatt,

> The imported material found in the Hallstatt graves shows trading connections with Etruria and Greece [two powerful ancient cultures], and with Rome as early as the third century B.C. The quantity of Italic metal imports is impressive; others come from Croatia-Slovenia. Amber [precious stones] points to communications with the north, and Egyptian influence may perhaps also be detected.[14]

Another indication that the Celts developed a trade network during the Hallstatt period comes from the land itself. The Hallstatt area is dominated by a salt mine, and many scholars believe that the Celts took possession of this mine and traded salt throughout the world. This enabled the Celts to develop a rich and wealthy society. According to Ross, "Hallstatt . . . consisted of a settlement with a flourishing local industry, that of salt-mining, and on this wealth the community depended. The huge cemetery [located in the area] testifies to the prosperity of the inhabitants."[15]

Throughout the Hallstatt period, the Celts continued to strengthen their culture and trade with other civilizations. Then sometime between about 500 and 400 B.C., the civilization shifted. There is no existing evidence that indicates how or why a change took place, but in that century the Celts seemed to go from an isolated, growing society to a fully formed civilization. This change can be seen in the artifacts from the next distinct period of Celtic history, the La Tène period.

The La Tène Culture

The second phase of the Celtic civilization occurred from about 400 to 1 B.C., immediately after the Hallstatt culture. Historians discovered this period of Celtic history by accident in 1858. That year, in the La Tène area of Switzerland on the shores of Lake Neuchâtel, low lake water revealed hundreds of blackened posts rising from the mud of the shore. Archaeologists investigated, and historian Barry Cunliffe describes what they uncovered: "Vast quantities of Iron Age metalwork were found: swords in their decorated sheaths, spears, shield bosses, horse gear, tools of all kinds together with ornaments, coins, and a host of other objects."[16]

This amazing find turned out to be a large Celtic settlement inhabited for about two or three hundred years around the fifth century B.C. Hundreds of artifacts were found buried in the mud of the lake bottom, revealing a new phase in Celtic culture.

The finds at La Tène were so significant that the place-name eventually became the name of that period in history. The artifacts showed a refinement in art, technology, and warfare from the earlier Hallstatt period. Most significantly, they showed a jump in art and craftsmanship, which would eventually become a trademark of the Celtic civilization.

The great advance in artistic skill was not the only hallmark of the La Tène period. Throughout Europe, archaeologists were finding other Celtic burial sites, similar to those found in Switzerland, that dated to around the same time. This suggested that it was a period of great expansion for the civilization.

This silver chalice from the La Téne period shows refined and advanced artistic skill.

There is little evidence as to why the Celts chose to migrate throughout Europe at this time. Some theories suggest that they had simply grown too large for northern Europe. Others maintain that an economic and social collapse forced the Celts to seek new lands in the west. Regardless, it is certain that by about 400 B.C. hundreds of thousands of Celtic men, women, and children flowed southward through the Alps and into the European landscape. Eventually, many of them moved on to England, Scotland, and Ireland, where the Celtic civilization would thrive, almost unchanged, until the advent of Christianity.

Difficulty in Reconstructing Celtic History

Despite all the information that exists about the once-great Celtic civilization, there is much more that is lost or missing. Historians have a very difficult time reconstructing details about the Celtic culture for a number of reasons.

The first problem is that a vast majority of the existing evidence consists of burial objects. Although these objects can tell historians quite a bit about some aspects of Celtic culture—such as the level of technology, artistic style, and migration patterns—they cannot tell how the objects were made, or where, or by whom. For example, it is clear from the amount of Celtic iron weapons that their civilization was advanced in metal-working and warfare during the La Tène period. But no one knows how the Celts acquired the technology or how it developed within their culture.

Second, the Celts were not a civilization with a written language and centers of culture. Instead, they were bands of tribes who shared a similar spoken language and common history. They never coalesced into one, singular organized culture. The Celtic tribes were eventually either wiped out or integrated into other cultures. Slowly, the achievements of the Celtic peoples were lost and forgotten as more powerful cultures supplanted them.

DESCRIPTION OF THE CELTS

Few descriptions of the Celtic people have survived, and the ones that do exist mainly in the form of accounts from ancient Roman and Greek writers. Many of these writers, especially the Roman commander Julius Caesar, described the Celts in battle. Others, such as the historian Diodorus Siculus, described their appearance, as David McCullough recounts in his book *Chronicles of the Barbarians*.

"The Gauls [Celts] are tall of body, with rippling muscles, and white of skin, and their hair is blond, and not only naturally so but they also make it their practice by artificial means to increase the distinguishing color which nature has given it. For they are always washing their hair in lime-water and they pull it back from their forehead to the top of the head and back to the nape of the neck, with the result that . . . the treatment of their hair makes it so heavy and coarse that it differs in no respect from the mane of horses. Some of them shave the beard, but others let it grow a little; and the nobles shave their cheeks, but they let the moustache grow until it covers the mouth. Consequently, when they are eating, their moustaches become entangled in the food, and when they are drinking, the beverage passes, as it were, through a kind of strainer."

Third, and most importantly, the Celts left no written records of their own civilization to teach historians about their culture. They chose to communicate with other civilizations orally, and their religious beliefs prohibited them from writing things down in their own language. They felt that the most powerful people were those who kept knowledge in their heads, and because of this they strove for personal knowledge over written records.

Furthermore, the records that do exist were written by their enemies, mainly the Romans. The Romans hated them and went to great lengths to make sure that the Celts were shown in the worst possible light. Peter Berresford Ellis explains this hatred, saying

> The defeat of the Roman army at Allia . . . left an indelible racial hatred towards the Celts. No other people encountered by Rome were viewed with such bigotry and intolerance nor described with such venom and repugnance. The root of this was that Rome feared the Celts. . . . The Roman writers invariably painted the Celts as one step above the animal.[17]

As a result of all these factors, the Celtic civilization eventually faded and disappeared. Long after they were gone, their reputations as bloodthirsty savages lingered. Since they left no other records of themselves, it was easy for history to remember them the way that the Romans portrayed them. It has been only in the last few decades that the Celts have emerged from the shadows to reclaim their rightful place as one of the greatest civilizations the world has ever seen.

CHAPTER TWO

TRIBES AND CHIEFTAINS

One of the hallmarks of the Celtic civilization was their desire to acquire and settle new areas. This was vital to the culture, and it is partly because of this attitude that they left the comfortable safety of their northern lands around 400 B.C. At that time, the Celts emerged from the Alps and swept through the Po valley, now modern-day Italy.

They continued on, eventually inhabiting most of Europe. They fought and traded with the Greek and Roman cultures. Historians, travelers, and army commanders wrote about them. The Celts established thriving communities and strongholds from Italy to Ireland. They were feared and hated by their enemies for their strange ways and their ferocious fighting style. However, their culture was eventually wiped out, and one reason for this was that the Celts, while a powerful group, never coalesced into an organized civilization.

No Organized Culture

The Celts were in fact a disparate group of tribal bands rather than a single culture. Although the tribes spoke the same form of the Celtic language, individual tribes, each with their own names and specific customs, settled throughout Europe. They established their own local chiefdoms, which consisted of their own lands and were separate from other groups in the area. Some tribes grew

rich and powerful, while others disappeared, victims of warfare and conquest.

As a result of this division, there were no great cities, no great centers of Celtic society. Cities are important to a civilization because they are a place where learning, commerce, politics, and society can flourish and grow. Although the Celts did have a number of large towns where commerce thrived, they were usually populated by specific tribes who controlled them. As historian Nora Chadwick attests, the Celts may have purposefully chosen not to establish large urban areas, although researchers are not certain why. She says, "The idea of urban life . . . appears to have been both foreign and repugnant to the Celts."[18]

Because the Celts never established cities, individual tribes became paramount. The tribes existed together and yet apart, farming their own lands, worshipping their gods, and warring with each other and with other groups that crossed their paths. They never joined forces to defeat their enemies or establish a unified culture, and this also kept them from achieving great power as a civilization.

Nor did the Celts ever establish a uniform government. Most Celtic tribes followed similar rules and laws, such as having kings and nobles in their groups, but those laws were binding only to the people who lived in that particular tribe. If an individual from one tribe left the group, he was at the mercy of the laws and traditions of any other tribe he came in contact with. Kings or chieftains had sovereignty over only the members of their own groups but no control over any other tribe beyond their borders. Although some Celtic tribes did band together to form large groups, even the largest tribes had no power over any other.

The fiercely independent Celtic spirit contributed to this lack of a central government. The Celts believed in loyalty to individuals, not to organizations, and their tribal systems were based in large part on personal fealty (loyalty to one leader) and respect of

PRINCELY GRAVE OF A CELTIC KING

Many Celtic graves have come to light, but none have been as magnificent as the rich grave of one Celtic leader, found near the German village of Hochdorf. This Celtic king's name was not recorded, but it is clear that he was a very important person in society.

He was buried sometime between 540 and 520 B.C. in a great mausoleum that was likely built just for him. It had two chambers made from huge oak beams. The king, who was about forty years old when he died, lay on a bronze, high-backed couch decorated with dancing figures. The legs of the couch were bronze figures of dancing girls who were mounted on wheels like delighted unicyclists. The chieftain was covered with garlands of late summer flowers.

His people dressed him in fine clothing made of richly embroidered Chinese silk. Around his neck, they placed a gold collar, amber beads, and a small bag that contained a toiletry kit of nail clippers, a razor, and a comb. His cloak was fastened with gold brooches, and he wore a gold armlet. A golden dagger hung at his belt, and his shoes were decorated with strips of gold.

He was also buried with a sturdy cart with four iron-covered wheels, draped with bronze chains and figures. It was piled with bowls, plates, platters, and knives—objects for feasting and celebration. Large drinking horns hung on the walls of the chamber, seemingly in wait for the guests to the feast. In one corner, sat a large bronze cauldron that had been filled with sweet honey mead, an alcoholic drink of the Celts.

The Celts clearly loved and respected this leader. They equipped him with everything he needed to live in the afterlife and to celebrate with his loyal comrades.

Celtic chieftans ruled only over their specific tribe. This illustration shows Celtic chieftans in their native dress of the 7th century A.D.

their own families. Because of this lack of a focused governmental structure, it was difficult for the Celts to organize and agree on a course of action, whether it was growing crops or waging war.

Along with their lack of a centralized government, the tribes did not follow an organized military structure. Although the Celts were reputed to be fierce and wild in battle, they were also very disorganized. Most Celtic armies, especially those in which a number of tribes banded together to fight a common enemy, had no overall commander or battle strategy. Instead, individual warriors followed their own tribal leader, who might or might not decide to work with other leaders to plan a defense or attack. This disorganization in battle created an atmosphere of chaos that, in many cases, frightened their enemies into defeat. However, other enemy commanders

such as the Roman Julius Caesar realized this and were able to crush the Celtic tribes, group by group.

Despite these weaknesses, the Celts were, for centuries, one of the most powerful groups in the world. During that time, individual tribes achieved great glory and power, and through them the Celtic civilization thrived.

Celtic Tribes in Europe

It is unclear exactly when the Celts established their groups in the various parts of Europe, although it is certain that they had been settled long before they sacked Rome in 390 B.C. According to Roman historians, the Celts entered Europe in a rush that lasted only a few years. However, most historians now agree that the Celtic tribes migrated slowly, over centuries. As Ellis points out,

The Celtic settlements south of the Alps were obviously not just one single movement of people, as Roman historians paint it, but several movements spread over several centuries. Their settlements were well established by the time of Allia. We can disagree with the early writers' perception that the migration of the Celts into Italy, and the capture of Rome, happened within a short space of time as one continuous movement.[19]

No records exist to help historians understand how and when the Celts settled in particular areas. Also, there is no information as to the size, population, or structure of most Celtic tribes, although historians speculate that more than one million Celts lived in the Po valley of Italy alone by 225 B.C.

What researchers do know is that by the time Roman and Greek writers began mentioning the Celts, the culture had already established itself in many parts of Europe. Although historians have little written information to tell them about the people, these ancient researchers did record where the Celtic tribes lived, such as areas of Gaul, Italy, and Great Britain. As Ellis explains, "We can be certain that, at the time when the Senones won their victory at Allia, the northern region of Italy had already become largely Celtic-speaking and an integral part of the La Tène cultural world of the Celts."[20]

Celts in Italy

The Po valley in Italy was one of the main areas in which the Celts settled as they began their migration westward. Many ancient historians mention this, and Celtic place-names in the area point to a large Celtic population

One million Celts had established themselves in the Po Valley of Italy by 225 B.C.

in this part of Italy. In addition, three now-famous Italian towns began as Celtic strongholds. Ancient historians wrote that a Celtic group called the Cenomani founded what was to become the modern city of Verona. This tribe must have been very powerful in the area, according to historian Ellis, for even their name implies strength and might, "This name comes from *cauraros*, a hero, as in the Old Irish *caur* meaning a giant, and *renos* meaning sea or waters."[21]

A tribe of Celts called the Boii took over an old town called Felsina and renamed it Bononia, which was to become modern-day Bologna. They were reputed to be the largest Celtic tribe in the Po valley at the time.

A third tribe, called the Veneti, lived east of the Po valley. Some scholars believe that this mighty group founded the modern-day city of Venice. The Veneti were a seafaring people who managed to convince a number of neighboring Celtic tribes to join with them in a battle against the Romans. According to historian Chadwick, the Roman commander Julius Caesar was impressed by the Veneti, saying that

> their state was by far the most powerful of any of that sea-coast because of both their expert seamanship and their fleet, in which they were accustomed to sail to Britain. . . . They controlled the ports and almost the entire trade of that open and stormy coast, and that they had as tributaries almost all those who were accustomed to sail the sea.[22]

Many other Celtic tribes populated northern Italy as well. The Insubres established their capital in Mediolanum, which means "central sanctuary." The Carni gave their name to the mountain range Alpi Carniche. The Lingones established their tribe in the Po delta near the Adriatic Sea. Others, such as the Libui, the Salassi, the Ananes, the Vertamocori, and the Leoponti, also lived in the area. It is clear by their sheer numbers that the Celts were a strong presence in Italy.

Celts in Gaul

Other Celtic tribes thrived in Gaul, an area that now includes modern-day France and Belgium. More is known about these Celts, because Julius Caesar wrote many descriptions of them in his book *The Gallic War*. At that time, Gaul was divided into large Celtic groups called *civitas*. A *civitas* consisted of all the territory of one group, and each group

had its own name, king, and customs. Some even had tribal centers, a few of which eventually gave their names to modern cities. Paris, for example, was believed to be the tribal center of the Celtic Parisi.

Civitates were further divided into smaller groups known as *pagi*. A *pagus* was a group of Celtic warriors who had joined together in battle. After a victory, these men were granted land for their families to settle on. A Celtic tribe might consist of a number of *pagus* groups linked by family and successful warfare. For example, historian Chadwick says, "Caesar tells us that the Hellvetti [tribe] were divided into four groups or *pagi*. Among the Aedui [tribe] at least six are known."[23]

By the time Caesar invaded Gaul in 58 B.C., five major Celtic tribes lived throughout the area: Redones, Namnetes, Venetes, Coriosolites, and Osismii. Other powerful tribes included the Celtae, Aquitani, Belgae, Attebates, Catuvellauni, Aedui, Bituriges, Carnutes, Arverni, Sequani, and the Allobroges. They spoke Celtic languages, and many of them battled against Caesar as he sought to conquer the land. However, almost no specific information exists about these tribes except their names. Although classical writers discussed the customs and lifestyles of the Gauls in detail, they speak only of the "Gauls" in general. They do not point to specific tribes as the source of their information.

Celts in Ireland

Ireland was populated by Celts from an early time, but almost nothing is known about the tribes that lived there. In the earliest days of the Celtic civilization, the land was divided into as many as one hundred chiefdoms or kingdoms, which were occupied by groups of people called *tuaths* (the people). At the beginning of the historical period, classical writers recorded the Celtic kingdoms in Ireland as Ailech, Airgialla, Ulaid, Munster, Ossory, Cashel, Meath, and Brega. Other than this sketchy information, little is known about the Celtic tribes who migrated to the island in the earliest days of Irish history.

Despite the disparate groups and lack of concrete information, historians do agree that Celtic tribes shared many common traits. Each one had a leader, for example, and the government of most Celtic tribes was based on a simple class system that included royalty, intellectuals, warriors, and farmers.

The Royals

Celtic royalty included the king, or chieftain, of a tribe and his family. The king's duties included serving as the leader of the tribe and conducting warfare and rituals. His religious duties sometimes took precedence over his exploits in battle, as Powell relates, "In pagan times the ritual functions of the king were of as great importance as were his executive ones in the assembly or on the battlefield."[24]

A Celtic king was elected by the kin of the former king, and sons did not always replace a father who had been king. Instead, Celtic rulers were elected based on their power, honor, integrity, and strength. But once a king achieved the throne, he was king for life, unless something such as sickness or injury made him unfit to rule.

In some cases, the king of a small tribe might be bound by personal allegiance to an overlord who ruled over a larger territory. This overlord had no authority over the lesser king's tribe, but he might help the lesser king

KING ARTHUR: CELT?

Legends of King Arthur and his knights of the Round Table have gripped imaginations for centuries. Although the romantic stories are mostly fiction, many historians believe that there was a great Arthur, and that he was a Celt.

This Celt probably lived in Britain sometime in the fifth century A.D. He could have been a warrior named Artorius, who was born about A.D. 470. Artorius was a skilled horseman and warrior who led small Celtic armies in battle. A few ancient sources mention such a warrior who died in battle. One of the most intriguing clues comes from a set of poems called the *Gododdin*. They were probably written about A.D. 600, and they describe a warrior named Arthur as a man of great honor and courage.

Although there is no proof that he was Artorius, these poems shows that British legend already included a great Celtic hero named Arthur. As a result, many historians suspect that storytellers used the Artorius legend as a basis for the King Arthur stories.

in times of war or famine. Very little is known about this arrangement, but historian Chadwick suggests that, "Theoretically . . . and no doubt practically, the inferior king gave hostages [taken from battle] to his overlord and perhaps received from him a stipend in token of his dependence. This probably amounted to service in time of war, and there is no certain evidence of any other form of mutual obligation."[25]

Equites, Druides, and Plebs

Below the king, Celtic society was divided into what the Romans referred to as *equites*, *druides*, and *plebs*. The *equites* were the Celtic nobility, which included the warrior class, the landowners, and patrons of the arts. The *druides*, or the intellectuals, made up another social class that was equal to the nobility in tribal status. This class of Celts included all the professional occupations such as judges, doctors, and astrologers. The best-known members of this class, however, were the Celtic priests whom the Romans also called druides. Bards, who were storytellers; *vates*, who were philosophers; and artisans, who created the beautiful jewelry and objects of the Celts, were also part of the *druide* class.

These intellectuals were especially revered by the Celts, who honored learning and intelligence as much as warfare. Of all of the Celtic intellectuals, the bards, druids, and *vates* were held in the highest esteem.

GAULS.

Celtic warriors were members of a class the Romans called equites *which included landowners and patrons of the arts.*

The third class of Celts, the *plebs*, consisted of freemen, minor craftsmen, and farmers. Although these people were considered to be the lower class, they made up the foundation of Celtic society. Almost nothing is known about this group, but it is likely that they played a major role in the Celtic civilization.

Although every member of a Celtic tribe was important, the vitality and structure of a particular group revolved around the king. To the Celts, their king was, literally, the life of the people and the very soul of the tribe. He represented their link with the land and its power to give life or death. His strength, power, and will could lead the Celts to unimaginable wealth and victory—or to complete defeat and death.

Kings Considered to be Divine

The Celts considered their kings to be sacred, part of the group of divine gods they worshipped. Although the king was chosen by the kin of the former king, the Celts believed that he was destined to be leader. Members of the tribe, they believed, were directed by the gods through magic and ritual to choose wisely. Consequently, the king they chose was the one that the gods had also chosen.

As a result, the king was a mystical being, descended from the gods and invested with kingship by the gods themselves. As Ross explains, "The king in Celtic society, as elsewhere, was believed to be a sacred, semidivine being; his ultimate ancestor was the . . . tribal god. He was of immense importance to the moral and physical well-being of his people."[26]

In the earliest days of the Celtic civilization, the king was the ultimate religious figure in the tribe. He served not only as priest but also as war leader, judge, and lawgiver. Slowly, the Celtic culture changed. By the time the earliest accounts of Celtic society were written during the first century A.D., a special group of priests, the druides, had assumed the religious functions of the king. In the years that followed, the king no longer conducted religious ceremonies, but his position as the highest religious member of the tribe remained.

The Celts believed their king was the personification of the life of the people. His physical well-being was believed to mirror the health of the tribe and to be magically tied to the health of the land—which in turn gave them life as well. As a result, many religious taboos sprang up around the kingship.

For example, no man who was physically imperfect in any way could become king. If the king fell ill or was injured in battle, he

A member of the Druide class wears a judicial habit. Druides acted, among other things, as judges in Celtic society.

could be judged unfit to rule. For the Celts, a weak or disfigured king could mean disaster. This is shown in one Celtic legend in which a Celtic king named Nuada had his hand cut off in battle. The mystical god of medicine, Dian Cecht, made Nuada a new hand out of silver. The hand was perfect in every way. However, the king was no longer fit to rule, and the Celts removed him from the kingship. Ross explains this theory, saying, "If the king . . . failed in any aspect of the qualities it was desirable he should possess, he must go, no matter how good a ruler he might be, or how beloved of his people."[27]

Kings Must be Fair

Truth and justice were also powerful, divine forces that were important to Celtic people. They believed that the king's honesty was a magical force that had the power to heal or destroy the tribe and the land. As Dillon and Chadwick relate, "The king was bound too by the magic power of Truth; and if he was guilty of injustice, disaster might overtake his people."[28]

Truth had many meanings for the Celts. It meant that a person was honest and did not lie to the people. It also meant that the king was fair. A good king dealt with people fairly and did not punish them overly harshly. One Celtic story illustrates the power of truth for the Celtic people. According to Irish legend, King Lugaid passed a judgment on a man whose sheep had grazed in the queen's garden. He forced the man to hand over the animals as punishment. Suddenly, the side of the king's house fell down the slope. Historians Dillon and Chadwick continue the story, saying,

> A young man named Cormac said, "No, the shearing of the sheep is enough in compensation for the grazing . . . for both will grow again." The house stayed and fell no further. "That is the true judgment," said all, "and it is the son of the true prince who has given it." For a year afterwards, Lugaid remained king . . . and no grass came out of the ground, nor leaves on the trees nor grain in the corn. Then the men of Ireland expelled him from the kingship, for he was a false prince; and Cormac became king.[29]

This story illustrates the Celts' overwhelming belief in the king as a divine power capable of controlling the land through truth. The land became barren, and the house could not stand because of an unfair king. The fair judgment by an honest man kept the house from falling, and it was this man whom the Celtic people wanted as their leader.

Ritual and Myth Joined the King With the Land

The physical fitness of the king was only a part of his divine power as ruler. The hundreds of beliefs and rituals that surrounded the kingship also had to be faithfully obeyed, or it could mean disaster. Powell clearly illustrates this belief when he says,

> The welfare of the tribe was also considered to be dependent on the ritual success of its king. . . . The failure of crops, cattle disease, or other misfortunes might be attributed to the supernatural unacceptability of the king resultant, in all probability, from some physical or ritual blemish, especially in regard to the numerous sanctions and observances that beset his every action.[30]

Most of these rituals included the king interacting with the gods of the land to ensure the health and prosperity of the Celtic people. They were symbolic statements that showed the king was one with the land and with the gods.

The most important Celtic kingship ritual was the king's ritualistic joining with the land during his inauguration ceremony. During the ceremony, the king had to symbolically marry the powerful goddess, Medb (Maeve), whom the Irish Celts also refered to as the sovereignty of Ireland. It was believed that only the man who joined with her could be king.

This symbolic marriage took many different forms, but the point was the same—to

BOUDICCA: WARRIOR QUEEN

Women in Celtic civilization had more freedom than in other societies, and some Celtic women rose to become fearsome warriors and queens in their own right. The most famous Celtic queen was Boudicca, and she led a rebellion against the Romans that would be remembered for centuries.

Boudicca, whose name means victory, was the widow of Prasutagus, the king of the Iceni tribe of Celts in Britain. The Iceni, a rich and refined tribe, were allied with Rome. In about A.D. 60 Prasutagus died, and he left half of his wealth to Rome and half to his two teenage daughters. When Roman agents came to collect their portion of Prasutagus's fortune, Boudicca and the Iceni greeted them with courtesy and Celtic hospitality. In return, the Romans turned on the people, seizing property and taking Celts as slaves. When Boudicca protested this harsh treatment, Romans whipped her publicly and raped her daughters. Boudicca and the Iceni were enraged. With terrifying speed, Boudicca led her people into war against the Romans.

Boudicca and the Celts ravaged the Romans: they destroyed Roman armies sent to subdue them and burned the Roman town of Colchester to the ground. Then Boudicca and the Celts turned to London, the center of Roman trade and finance in Britain. The Celts smashed through London, destroying it.

After these humiliations, the Romans mustered their forces and finally defeated Boudicca and the Celts. Little is known of Boudicca's fate after the rebellion. Some say she took poison rather than be taken prisoner by the Romans. Other accounts say she died of sickness and was buried by her people. Regardless, she remains a symbol of Celtic power and freedom.

show that the king and the land were one. This ritual, a fertility rite, was meant to ensure that the land and the people would prosper during the king's reign.

During the ritual, an animal, usually a mare, represented Medb. Throughout the ceremony, the king performed various rites, after which the mare was sacrificed. The Celts thought that the blood and flesh of an animal—part of the natural world—held magical powers. Those who ate the flesh of certain animals, especially animals that symbolized particular gods or goddesses, would acquire great power. The ceremony was described by an ancient historian named Giraldus Cambrensis, who wrote,

He who is to be inaugurated . . . comes before the people on all fours. The mare being immediately killed and cut into pieces and boiled, a bath is prepared for him from the broth. Sitting in this he eats the flesh which is brought to him, the people standing round and partaking of it also. He is also required to drink the broth in which he is bathed. . . . These . . . things being duly accomplished, his royal authority and domination are ratified.[31]

Some historians dismiss this description, suggesting that Cambrensis was trying to cast the Irish as inhuman brutes. Others believe that he accurately described an ancient Celtic practice that survived for hundreds of years, and many Irish legends include descriptions of similar ceremonies. Scholars believe that the myths, taken together, echo the actual beliefs of the Celts and the religious ceremonies they used to bring their rulers to power.

Choosing the Right King

It was vitally important that the Celts choose the right kings. If a weak or dishonest king were chosen, he could destroy the land and the people. Therefore, the Celts had many rituals to ensure that they chose the man destined to be king.

One such ritual concerned the druides and animal sacrifice. When a new king was needed for the tribe, a bull was slaughtered. A druid ate the flesh and drank a broth made from the animal. Then, according to Ellis, "He [the druid] went into a meditative trance, while four others chanted over him, and he was thought to receive a vision of the next true king."[32]

Another way that the Celts chose their kings was by using sacred stones. One of

the most powerful Celtic beliefs was that natural objects such as water, stone, and wood are imbued with magical forces. The Celts believed that certain stones had supernatural powers that could reveal the true king.

Special stones were used at many inauguration ceremonies, for it was thought that these stones would cry out when the foot of the true king touched them. The most famous stone was known as Lia Fail, or the Stone of Destiny. It was housed at the great Celtic stronghold of Tara in Ireland. According to ancient legend, the Stone of Destiny shrieked when any true king of Ireland stood upon it. One colorful Celtic story says that, "When the High King, Conn of the Hundred Battles, stepped on to [the Stone of Destiny], it uttered a number of shrieks. These were interpreted by the Druids as representing the number of Conn's descendants who would be kings of Ireland."[33]

Celtic kings were regarded as mystical by their people, but they were also very human. Their words and actions had serious consequences upon their people and the natural world around them.

The Celtic kings were the leaders of a culture that grew and flourished for more than four hundred years. There is little evidence that sheds light on the details of Celtic life, but it is clear that the civilization was a powerful force in Europe. Although individual tribes never joined to create one all-encompassing Celtic civlization, their culture infused Europe with new ideas. Hundreds of Celtic tribes migrated and settled the landscape during this time, bringing their unique beliefs, language, and culture to the ancient world.

CHAPTER THREE

MASTERS OF SCIENCE AND TECHNOLOGY

If ancient historians are to be believed, the Celts had few redeeming qualities, especially when it came to technology and science. These writers insisted that the great Celtic civilization was little more than a disorganized group of warriors with no desire to do anything but fight and hunt. Farming was the last thing on their minds, according to some Romans.

This distorted view could not be farther from the truth. In fact, modern research has revealed that the Celts were skilled farmers and craftsmen, and they revered the land. In fact, they devised new tools and developed agricultural methods that laid the foundation for European economic growth for centuries to come.

Iron: A Superior Metal

As the Celts moved throughout Europe in the last millennium B.C., great changes were happening in the world—most notably, the move from the Bronze to the Iron Age. Iron was replacing bronze in the manufacture of weapons and tools. All over Europe, people were beginning to use iron because it is much stronger and more durable than bronze. The Celts were at the center of this technological revolution. According to his-

torian Ellis, "Iron tools and weapons rendered the Celts superior to their neighbors and were doubtless the basis of their sudden eruption throughout Europe at the beginning of the first millennium B.C."[34]

Some scholars speculate that the Celts were among the first northern Europeans to embrace iron and use it to their advantage. They replaced their bronze swords with deadlier blades of iron and became even more fearsome in battle. They improved agricultural equipment by creating farming tools that were superior to any others then used in Europe. As a result, many Celtic villages became valuable as exporters, selling their crops, tools, and animals throughout the world.

Iron Working

The use of iron did not sweep through Europe in one quick wave. It was a gradual change that happened over centuries. Although the Celts were not the only civilization to use the new metal, they were among the first to realize its power.

Iron did not alter life for the Celts much in the beginning. In the early years of Celtic society, iron was used mainly to decorate bronze objects such as swords. But slowly, the Celts began using iron more and more, and archaeological digs throughout Europe have unearthed Celtic villages that included iron-smelting centers. The tribes living in modern-day Poland, for example, had a thriving iron industry during the La Tène period, about the first century A.D. Authors Françoise Andouze and Olivier Buchsenschutz describe this industry,

> The Holy Cross Mountains [in Poland] are riddled with batteries [collections] of low-shaft furnaces partly dug into the ground. At Biskupice, south-east of Warsaw, the ore from the river terraces was mined in trenches perpendicular to the river. The furnaces were grouped together in a separate part of the settlement here, but the work of forging [making iron tools] took place in the houses [of the settlement] themselves.[35]

By the middle of the La Tène period, iron had spread throughout Celtic Europe and was being used in innovative ways. The Celts used iron for a variety of ordinary objects such as nails and tools for working bone and wood. No other culture in the world at the time used iron in this way. Even the most advanced civilizations of the ancient world, such as Rome and Greece, had yet to discover how useful the metal was. The Celts' widespread use of iron gave them a huge advantage over other cultures and demonstrates that they were, in this area, more technologically advanced than other cultures. Andouze and Buchsenschutz mention that even the Roman commander Julius Caesar noticed this, "Caesar notes, for example, that the anchors of the ships of the Veneti were attached with

The Celts widespread use of iron, such as the battle axes shown here, demonstrates that, in this area, they were more technologically advanced than other cultures of the time.

iron chains, whereas at that time the Romans were still using ropes."[36]

Where Did the Knowledge Come From?

Ironworking represented the greatest technological advancement for the Celtic civilization, but how they made this remarkable achievement remains a mystery. There is no evidence to say how they acquired the knowledge of metalworking; however, scholars do offer some ideas. According to Ellis, "It may simply be that they developed [their proficiency in ironworking] through the process of working other metals. . . . The Celts, experimenting over many centuries with smelting and forging techniques, probably arrived at their knowledge without outside influence."[37]

Regardless of how the Celts came by this new technology, they used it to their advantage. Ultimately, the agricultural tools they wrought from iron had a tremendous impact on the world.

Advances in Farm Tools

For centuries the Celts were perceived to be a migrant band of warlike tribes that wandered throughout Europe. Caesar scoffed, "They do not pay much attention to agriculture, and a large portion of their food consists in milk, cheese, and flesh, nor has any one a fixed quantity of land."[38]

But in recent years, historians and archaeologist have been able to prove that the Celts were highly successful farmers. According to Ellis,

Archaeology disproves the popular notion of the Celts being an itinerant [moving] people, constantly travelling Europe in great hordes, attacking and looting as they went. Both agricultural and pastoral farming were practised and indeed became highly sophisticated as the Celts combined their technology with other rural knowledge and skills. . . . In fact, Celtic farmers, in whatever part of the ancient Celtic world they lived, could have taught the Romans a few lessons on farming.[39]

The basic tool of all farming at that time was the plow, a tool that digs and cuts the earth so that crops can be planted. But early plows were too primitive to dig effectively, so most European societies practiced double plowing, which entailed running the plow over a field twice to break the soil. This was difficult and time consuming.

To solve this problem, the Celts added a coulter, a sharp knife, to the plow beam. The coulter made a vertical cut through the soil at the same time as the blade of the plow, called a plowshare, made a horizontal cut. In this way, the soil was turned over in one pass.

This simple innovation drastically changed farming because fields could be plowed quickly and effectively. The Celts also began making their plowshares out of iron, even as other cultures continued using wooden plowshares. This combination of metal coulter and plowshare made the job of preparing fields for planting much easier. Ellis reports, "The iron provided the Celts with, literally, an 'edge' over their neighbors. The plow was often pulled by two yoked oxen and by this means they were able to open up vast tracts of arable land. The Celtic farmers would penetrate regions previously impossible to plow and cultivate."[40]

The Celts also began making smaller farming tools such as sickles, scythes, spades, forks, and axes out of iron. Iron made these simple tools powerful and sophisticated, making it possible for the Celts to cultivate and maintain much more land than other cultures. Even now, many modern farming implements closely resemble ancient Celtic tools, as Ellis says, "The hand tools which we still use today were all anticipated by Celtic craftsmen at least by the first century B.C." [41]

Inventing the *Vallus*

One of the Celts' most amazing innovations was the invention of what many historians consider to be the world's first harvesting machine. This machine, called *vallus* by the Romans, was unlike anything that had been seen before. It was unusual enough for Pliny, an ancient writer, to record a fairly detailed description of it. He said it was a "big box, the edges armed with teeth and supported by

THE COLIGNY CALENDAR

The druides were especially interested in astronomy, astrology, and the movements of the heavens. Through their knowledge of the stars, they were able to create their own highly accurate calendar.

This document, called the Coligny Calendar, consists of fragments of a huge bronze plate, engraved with a calendar of sixty-four consecutive lunar months. The document is written in the Celtic language, but the numbers and letters are Roman.

The calendar is unusual in that it measures time by night, not day as modern calendars do. In the book *Everyday Life of the Celts*, historian Anne Ross quotes Caesar describing this system, "They count periods of time not by the number of days but by the number of nights; and in reckoning birthdays and the new moon and the new year their unit of reckoning is the night followed by the day."

The calendar is made of a sophisticated cycle of lunar measurement and calculation. There are sixty-four months in the calendar divided into either twenty-nine or thirty nights each. It also divides the year into a dark half, or cold months, and a light half, or warm months. In the middle of these two halves of the year is a Celtic word, *atenvix*, which means renewal. It is unclear what this time of the year represented.

The Celts' reputation as respected astrologers continued for centuries. To most scholars, the existence of the Coligny Calendar proves that the Celts were a highly intelligent people who valued scientific learning.

two wheels, which moved through the corn-field pushed by an ox; the ears of corn were uprooted by the teeth and fell into the box."[42]

Other than this description, and a stone relief carving from Brussels, Belgium, show-ing such a machine, nothing else exists to give historians any insight into how the Celts developed, constructed, or used their harvesting machine. No existing examples of a Celtic harvesting machine have ever been found. However, archaeologists and scholars suspect that the Celts' *vallus* was another tool that gave them an agricultural edge over the rest of Europe.

Innovative Farming Techniques

The Celts' new iron tools and machines en-abled them to grow a large variety of crops. Depending on which area of Europe a par-ticular tribe lived in, the main crops would be wheat, millet, barley, rye, oats, or corn. They also grew flax, a plant from which linen fabric is made. Beans, peas, and lentils were not uncommon, and the Celts culti-vated many different kinds of fruits and berries, including grapes for wine.

The Celts planted many of their crops in what historians now call Celtic fields. These fields, probably developed during the Bronze Age, were widely used by the Celtic civilization, especially tribes in Great Britain. A Celtic field was, as Powell describes,

> rarely bigger than some four hundred by two hundred and sixty feet, and is frequently much smaller. The fields are more often rectangular than truly square, but their width is great in pro-portion to their length, and this was evidently intended to assist in plow-

ing both along and across the area within the boundaries.[43]

The Celts built hundreds of these small fields side by side, making their farms resem-ble a patchwork of small squares. The fields were separated by low earthen banks that helped control the humidity of the soil, a practice that improves the quality of the soil. The existence of these ancient Celtic fields illustrates two points: that the Celts were an important farming civilization and that they understood complex agricultural methods just as well as, if not better than, their con-temporaries. According to Andouze and Buchsenschutz,

> The "Celtic fields" show that, from the Bronze Age in England, there was a wish to improve the lands on which human groups had settled permanently. Building banks indicated the desire to control soil humidity and to prevent erosion or incursions by animals. It sug-gests the import of more fertile soil or manuring. This raises the possibility that these techniques were practised equally in all the cultivated areas.[44]

Celtic farming settlements usually con-sisted of individual farms and small villages scattered among the Celtic fields. Although no records exist that tell exactly how the Celts lived and worked on their farms, ar-chaeological evidence does suggest that these settlements hummed with life. Chad-wick describes the ancient farmsteads,

> Within a palisade or enclosing wall there were husking and winnowing places, granaries for seed corn, drying

Celtic farming settlements usually included individual plots of land that included fields, storage areas, and thatched houses like this one

racks for corn or hay, underground storage pits for grain, and perhaps one or more small buildings ancillary to the farmhouse. There might be one or more enclosures for livestock. . . . In some more highland areas, cattle corrals and enclosures of varied types may be recognized.[45]

The Role of Livestock

Just as important to the Celts was raising livestock. They had a variety of domesticated animals, including cattle, sheep, pigs, dogs, and horses. The Celts believed that these animals served many useful purposes in addition to the products they provided. Many of them were entwined in the Celtic belief that the natural world was filled with mystical powers. These animals were seen as

vital to the welfare of the Celtic people, part of the natural world that gave them life.

Cattle were by far the most important animals to the Celts. In the culture's rural society, cattle were a sign of wealth and social status for a Celtic family. Cattle provided milk and meat, and they were also used as draft animals to pull the heavy Celtic plows and wagons. Cattle also played a role in Celtic spiritual beliefs. Throughout Celtic art and mythology, cattle—especially bulls—appear frequently. To the Celts, bulls represented strength, fertility, and power, and a strong bull in a family's cattle herd was considered to be a great asset. According to Ellis, the Celts believed that bulls held special powers and were used in religious rituals, "Because of the importance of cattle in Celtic society, bulls played a major role in

Celtic culture. Images of bulls begin to appear in the Hallstatt culture and they are frequently connected with sacrificial rituals."[46]

Pigs, another common animal in the Celtic world, also played a large role in the spiritual life of the Celts. Pigs and boars had a special religious significance that isn't completely understood today, but archaeologists have noted that these animals were important enough to be included in rich Celtic graves. Celtic warriors wore symbols of boars on their helmets, and sculptures depicting pigs and boars are common in Celtic art. Early Irish kings adopted the boar as their royal symbol as well. Pigs also appear in many Celtic legends, suggesting that they were considered to be part of the spiritual, as well as the natural, world.

Not only were pigs a source of religious significance, they were also a lucrative export item. The Celts let their herds of pigs gorge themselves on acorns in early Europe's expansive oak forests and then sold the animals. At least three ancient writers, Polybius, Cato, and Strabo, commented on this, as Ellis points out,

> Polybius says that in his time the great oak forests were still extensive enough to provide acorns for fodder for vast herds of pigs. Cato was much impressed by the enormous flitches of bacon from pigs bred by the Insubreans [a Celtic tribe]. Strabo says that "the forests bear such an abundance of acorns that Rome is largely fed on the herds of Cisalpine [an area where many Celtic tribes lived] swine."[47]

Sheep, while not as religiously significant as cattle or pigs, also played a big role in Celtic agriculture. They provided wool, which the Celts exported to many parts of Europe. Caesar mentions that the Celts of Britain exported wool to Rome, and the ancient writer Strabo pointed out that "the wool trade . . . 'clothed the greater part of Italy' . . . soft wool from the Boii [a Celtic tribe] country, coarser fabric from the east of Cisalpine Gaul [an area inhabited by Celtic tribes] and costly carpets and woolen covers from around Patavium (Padua)."[48]

The woolen garments made from Celtic sheep continued to keep Europe warm for centuries. Even long after the Celtic civilization fell into decline, their farming traditions lingered in such areas as Scotland and Ireland. Even today, Irish and Scottish woolen fabrics are among the best in the world.

Although the Celtic civilization revolutionized European farming and agriculture, almost nothing remains of the people's great achievements. As authors Andouze and Buchsenschutz comment, "The Celts seem . . . to have colonized new territories over the whole of central Europe thanks to their superior technology, but one which has not left any spectacular material remains."[49]

Despite this, however, most scholars today agree that the Celts' use of advanced farming techniques and iron tools made an enormous contribution to Euroopean agriculture.

Medicine

But agriculture, was not the only area in which the Celts excelled. They were also a learned culture that was highly advanced in many scientific areas. Medicine, for example, was one of the Celts' areas of expertise, and they had been practicing advanced medical techniques long before Christian

TALE OF THE CELTIC WARRIOR-SURGEON

In 1996, archaeologists found a Celtic grave in the area of Colchester, England. Among the burial goods they uncovered was a set of surgical instruments.

These instruments were found in the tomb of a well-respected Celtic citizen who lived during the early years of Roman occupation of Britain, the third or early second century B.C. The medical kit he was buried with suggests that he was a healer in his tribe and that he practiced a wide variety of surgical techniques, including operations on tonsils and cataracts.

The kit consisted of thirteen instruments including scalpels, hooks, forceps, needles, and even a small saw. Although the tools look somewhat like Roman bronze medical instruments of the time, the Celtic tools are made of iron.

Archaeologists suspect that this Celtic doctor was probably a chieftain's personal physician, although they cannot say this for sure. What is certain, however, is that the Celts had a wide variety of medical knowledge and learning, and that they used sophisticated surgical instruments to care for the ailments of their people.

monks recorded them, recognizing that Celtic medical knowledge rivaled that of the rest of the ancient world. Ellis says, "In medicine, as in so many other areas, the Celts stand favorable in comparison with the classical world."[50]

One of the most interesting medical procedures the Celts practiced was a form of brain surgery called trephining. In this procedure, the physician makes a circular cut into the skull to relieve pressure that might have resulted from such things as battle wounds or other head injuries. This surgical technique is very delicate, and few patients could have survived it. The Celts were quite skilled at trephining, however, and archaeol-

ogists have found a number of ancient skulls with clean, circular holes cut into them. Many of these holes show signs of healing, suggesting that the patient not only survived the operation but lived on afterward.

A rare record of a trephining operation is included in a written account of the battle of Magh Rath in A.D. 637. In the account, an Irish chieftain named Cennfaelad suffered a severe head injury in battle. According to Ellis, "He was taken to the medical school of Tuam Brecain (Tomregan) and had the injured part of his skull and a portion of his brain removed. On his recovery, it was said that his wits were as sharp as ever and he became a great scholar and author."[51]

Celtic physicians were also skilled in medical botany, the understanding of the healing properties of plants. They produced herbal sleeping potions as well as some poisons, and they were also reputed to be knowledgeable about the mystical healing properties of mistletoe. Written accounts by ancient historians describe druides harvesting mistletoe from the tops of oak trees, and they usually suggest that this was some kind of magical rite. However, mistletoe has many healing properties, including benefits to people with insomnia and high blood pressure. The Celts may have understood these benefits and used mistletoe as a healing herb.

Hospitals were another influential Celtic innovation. In the ancient world, healing was generally reserved for the wealthy. Poor people who became sick were usually left to die or put to death. The Celts believed that all people, regardless of their station in life, should have a chance at healing. The first hospital in Ireland, called Broin Bherg (House of Sorrow) was said to have been established sometime in the fourth century B.C. by the Celtic queen Macha Mong Ruada. Irish legend describes this hospital as being in use until it was destroyed in A.D. 22 Although it is unclear whether this particular hospital actually existed, historians do know that hospitals like it were in existence in Ireland by the time of the Christian period. These hospitals gave medical attention to anyone who was ill, regardless of their place in society.

The Celts were also highly respected in the area of medical learning. Many Roman physicians were said to have studied at medical colleges in Gaul, and ancient writers such as Pliny mention the reputation of Celtic healers. Although few other details are known about Celtic medical practices, it is clear that Celtic physicians were regarded with respect by the rest of the world.

Astrology

In the classical world, astrology was considered to be a high form of knowledge. Many respected scholars studied the stars and the movement of the heavenly bodies, and mixed their learning with their beliefs in gods and the natural world. They used astrology to predict the future, to pray to their gods, and to aid in healing. The Celts were no exception. Numerous ancient writers mention the Celts' vast knowledge of the heavens, including Caesar, who in describing the druides, noted, "They . . . hold long discussions about the heavenly bodies and their movement, the size of the universe and of the earth, the physical constitutions of the world, and the power and properties of the gods."[52]

Unfortunately, historians do not really know what knowledge of the stars the Celts had. But it appears that they did have a sophisticated understanding of the universe, for they developed their own calendar system. They used a thirty-year cycle, naming the months and showing where they fell in the course of the year. They also measured time by the number of nights, not days, that passed. Their calendars were surprisingly accurate, demonstrating an advanced knowledge of the heavens.

The Hill-Forts

The Celts were also advanced in the field of architecture. Although most settlements consisted of small villages surrounded by farming fields, a few villages grew into large

Maiden Castle in Britain remained a celtic fortification until the Romans captured it in 44 A.D.

towns. Many of these towns sprang up near royal residences and became local centers for trade and commerce both within Celtic society and beyond its borders.

Some of these towns, called *oppida*, rivaled any other in the classical world. *Oppida* were well-organized towns, set on a pattern of streets with homes and businesses, usually enclosed by a strong earthen fortification. These structures dotted the European landscape. Andouze and Buchsenschutz described the magnificence of the *oppida*, also called hill-forts,

> The fortifications erected during the Bronze and Iron Ages constitute the most impressive group of monuments

that have come down to us from protohistory. Several thousand sites spread over the whole of Europe were laid out on a grand scale with the construction of banks and ditches, in order to provide defence for a human group or simply to affirm their power.[53]

These immense structures were masterworks of architectural skill. They were made of earth, stone, and timber, and many of them stretched for hundreds of acres. The Celts used a staggering number of materials to build such structures, suggesting that the hill-forts were carefully planned and executed over a long period of time. Only societies that were well settled and had enough

CELTIC CRANNOGS

Most Celts lived in small farming villages of a few houses surrounded by fields. However, in some places, Celtic villagers felt the need for more protection from enemies. They developed an ingenious method of construction that had not been seen before: the crannog.

A *crannog* is a house built on a large platform in the center of a lake or marshlands. This construction technique shows how the Celts solved a security problem with skill. First, Celtic builders chose a likely site. Then they floated large boulders to the center of the water and began piling them until they formed an island. The Celts also cut huge amounts of wood and added it to the growing artificial island. Once the island was large enough, they built a sturdy wooden platform on top of it. A house was built on the platform.

Once the house was finished, the Celts sometimes added a wooden walkway to shore, complete with a drawbridge to protect them from invaders. These houses, clearly meant to be permanent dwellings, are a creative example of the Celts' architectural skills.

resources and manpower could construct such grand *oppida*.

One of the most famous Celtic *oppidum* still exists in Britain. Called Maiden Castle, it was built sometime around 350 B.C. It continued to be a Celtic stronghold for more than four hundred years. In A.D. 44, Romans invaded Maiden Castle and killed all of the Celtic men, women, and children who lived there.

No information exists as to exactly how the Celts managed to build such grand structures. However, the existence of these *oppida* are a testament to the skill and in-

genuity of Celtic science and technology. Ellis praises the Celtic builders when he states,

> The excavation of these fortified towns or hill-forts leaves one openmouthed at the craftsmanship of the Celtic architects and builders. There are literally hundreds of hill-forts and thousands of ring-forts throughout the ancient Celtic world. The work involved in moving such colossal amounts of earth and stone is absolutely breath-taking.[54]

CHAPTER FOUR

RELIGION, MYTH, AND THE DRUIDS

The Celts were a highly religious people. Many ancient writers comment on this fact, suggesting that religion was very important to the Celtic civilization as a whole. Unfortunately, the Celts left no written records of their specific beliefs, and the secrets of their religion have been lost to history.

They did, however, have a rich history of myths and legends that told the stories of their gods and their interactions with heroes of Celtic history. Most of these stories were not written down until the Christian era, when Christianity supplanted pagan beliefs throughout Europe and Great Britain in the first centuries of the first millennium A.D. Many Celtic intellectuals, especially those in Ireland, embraced the new faith and became monks, but they were unwilling to let go completely of the ancient beliefs of their people. Since Christianity did not prohibit the writing of information, these new Celtic Christians began recording all the ancient stories.

But in doing so, they edited many of the old stories, adding Christian elements and weakening the power of the mighty pagan gods. For years, historians ignored these writings as mere stories with no historical importance. It has been only in the last few decades that researchers have realized the myths hold many clues to the workings of ancient Celtic religion.

Gods and Goddesses Were Part of the Natural World

It is clear from the stories that the civilization's religious belief was entwined with the workings of nature. For the Celts, gods and goddesses did not control nature, they lived within it. The mysterious earth, for example, was the source of all fertility and was watched over by great earth gods and goddesses. Gods inhabited rocks and mountains; they existed in the mighty rivers and small, bubbling springs; gods were part of the forests and the trees. Gods shapeshifted into powerful and mysterious animals such as the boar, the stag, and the raven.

But the Celts did not worship objects such as trees or rocks as deities. Specific things in nature were, to them, the manifestation of the god or goddess that lived within it. Natural objects symbolized the gods and goddesses, who in turn symbolized the power of nature. The earth goddess was not only a deity, for example; she was also the physical representation of the earth and its power to give life. Celtic scholar Miranda Green points out that,

"A very significant trait in Celtic religion . . . is the endowment with sanctity of natural features—a river, spring, lake, tree, mountain, or simply a particular valley or habitat. The gods were everywhere."[55]

Trees were especially revered by the Celts. Nemetona, the goddess of the grove, was an important deity, and many religious ceremonies were conducted in sacred tree groves. In Celtic mythology, trees stood as signposts to mystical places. In one story, a tree covered with silver flowers stood at the cave entrance to the Celtic Otherworld (the place where the gods lived and the dead sometimes visited), inhabited by the gods. Tribes adopted specific trees, and these trees became sacred

CELTIC HOLIDAYS

In the Celtic civilization, the natural world controlled much of daily life. Celts saw the passing years as being just another part of the natural world, filled with darkness and light, birth and death, warmth and cold. The gods and goddesses were there through it all.

To mark the two major turning points of the year, the Celts celebrated two major festivals. The greatest Celtic festival was Samhain, (pronounced SOW-an), observed on November 1 but celebrated on the night before. Samhain was the Celtic New Year. It was the end of the summer growing and grazing season, and the time when cattle and sheep were brought together and slaughtered.

Samhain was also a time between two years when Celts believed that spirits from the Otherworld could walk the earth. Magic was very powerful during this time as well, and many important rituals were conducted. Today, remnants of the Celtic beliefs can be seen in the Halloween celebrations that include spirits and ghosts.

The second most important Celtic celebration was Beltane. This holiday, celebrated on May 1, marked the arrival of the light months of spring and summer. It was a fertility celebration, filled with feasting and dancing. It also corresponded with the release of cattle for grazing in the fields. Today some people continue to celebrate May Day with gifts of flowers, and the tradition of dancing around a Maypole harks back to the ancient Celtic Beltane celebrations.

Within the Celtic belief system, the reverence for nature and its effect on their lives ran deep. The Celts honored this power with their holidays, all of which celebrated the gods and the natural world that gave them life.

to the people. Some tribes inaugurated their new kings beneath these sacred trees.

Animals and Metamorphosis

Animals also played a significant role in Celtic religion, but the Celts did not worship the animals themselves. Many gods and goddesses, they believed, could change into certain animals at will, and these animals came to represent the essence, or spirit, of a deity. Green explains this, "Just as the supernatural in natural features was acknowledged, so animals possessed a sanctity and divine element. . . . The relationship of human to animal images may be explained partly in the phenomenon of metamorphosis which plays such an important role in Celtic . . . tradition."[56]

The Celts believed strongly in the idea of metamorphosis. Many myths and legends tell of gods and goddesses who changed from their human shape into the forms of birds and animals. Usually, a god or goddess shapeshifted into the animal that represented special powers or religious beliefs associated with that deity. For example, the goddesses of war, the Morrigan, were believed to shapeshift into carrion-eating ravens. Since these black birds would swarm a field of battle and feast on the dead, the Celts believed this animal was a manifestation of their goddess of war and death.

This idea of metamorphosis illustrates the Celts' strong belief in the close associations between their gods and the natural world. To them, a crow flying overhead was more than a bird—it might also be a goddess, speeding away on some urgent errand. An angry, snorting boar was an animal, certainly, but it might also be an enraged god.

The Celts admired and respected animals for their speed, strength, cunning, courage, and ferocity. The gods, in turn, shared these traits. The bull, for example, as Delaney points out, "courses through Celtic mythology as a powerful symbol of strength, virility, sexuality, an object of wealth and desire and stature. The bull defended the herds from rustlers and thereby became a god of battle, since most warfare originated in search and defence of property, including sources of food."[57]

Holy Places in Nature

The Celts believed that the power of nature surged around them at all times. It could be seen not only in trees or animals but also in specific natural locations. As a result, they worshipped in holy places in nature that they believed were imbued with mystical powers.

In some areas, the Celts built simple enclosures open to the sky, in which to pray to their gods. But most of the time, they chose to worship in natural, sacred places. They believed these places had strong powers. One of the most powerful places in the Celtic world were areas associated with water.

In the ancient Celtic world, water was one of the mightiest forces in nature. The Celts understood that water was the basis of life. They revered water and its ability to give life to plants, animals, and people. As a result, powerful fertility goddesses were associated with water, and several rivers, lakes, and streams were sacred to the Celtic culture. The Celts bathed in these sacred waterways, and left offerings such as clothing, household objects, weapons, and farming tools in the water. Archaeologists have found thousands of these objects in lakes, rivers, and bogs all over Europe. The famous La Tène archaeological site, for example, was one such offering place. The Celts built a special wooden platform on Lake Neuchâtel and threw

A priest cuts mistletoe from a sacred tree as Roman soldiers look on. Trees were especially revered by the Celts.

offerings into the lake. Clearly, this place was especially holy to the Celts.

Because the Celts revered water, they gave goddess names to many European rivers. Many of these names survive today. Historian Ellis points to several rivers in Europe that have been named for Celtic goddesses, "The Marne, for example, comes from *Matrona*, which means 'mother'; the Severin in Britain is named after Sabrina. . . . The Boyne in Ireland is named after the goddess Boann; while the Shannon takes its name from the goddess Siannon. . . . Sequana was the goddess of the Seine."[58]

Many of these goddesses are associated with fertility and healing, suggesting that the Celts viewed the rivers as a source of these powers. They also considered smaller bodies

of water, such as springs, to be just as healing and powerful as the great rivers. Sacred Celtic springs can be found throughout Europe. Many of them are thermal or mineral springs, which the Celts believed had great healing properties. People would travel great distances to soak in and drink from the healing springs and to give offerings to the goddesses who controlled them. Visitors who were ill made small replicas of the affected body part—legs, arms, eyes, heads—and cast them into the water. They made these offerings, says Green, "Either as a reminder to the goddess as to what required treatment or so as to transfer magically their ills from themselves to the model."[59]

Many of these sacred water-places, especially the springs, were considered holy for years after the Celtic civilization declined. Over the years, Roman deities replaced the Celtic ones, but people continued to worship their gods at these special places.

Sacred Tree Groves

Another holy place in nature was the sacred tree groves. Many ancient writers mention the sacred groves of the Celtic people, and trees play a large part in many Celtic myths. However, there is little archaeological evidence to link the Celts with specific groves of trees. The strongest evidence as to the importance of groves to the Celts comes in the language and place-names of sites throughout Europe.

The Celtic word *nemeton*, for example, which denotes a sacred grove, is also the name of the goddess Nemetona (goddess of the grove). The word is found throughout Celtic Europe in other place-names such as *Drunemetion* (the oak sanctuary), which was, according to the ancient writer Strabo, the meeting place of the Galatians, a tribe of

THE DRUIDS AND THE WRITTEN WORD

One of the most mysterious features of the Celts was their belief that it was unlawful to commit their learning to writing in their own language. Many historians interpreted that belief to mean that the Celts were illiterate. On the contrary, they were a very literate people. They used Greek and Latin to write many things, including personal and business transactions. However, their scholarly learning and religious teachings were sacred and could not be written down.

This curious fact interested many ancient writers, including Julius Caesar. In his book *Chronicles of the Barbarians*, editor David McCullough relates Ceasar's description of how the druids committed their knowledge to memory and why he thought the druids refused to use written language.

[The druids] . . . learn by heart a great number of verses; accordingly some remain in the course of training for twenty years. Nor do they regard it lawful to commit these to writing. . . . That practice they seem to me to have adopted for two reasons; because they neither desire their doctrines to be divulged among the mass of people, nor those who learn, to devote themselves . . . less to the efforts of memory . . . since it generally occurs to most men, that, in their dependence on writing they relax their diligence in learning it [knowledge] thoroughly.

Celts; *Nemetodurum* and *Nemetacum* in Gaul, and *Nemtogriga* in Spanish Galicia. In Britain, a place called *Vernemetion*, which means the especially sacred grove, is recorded in Roman times. *Medionemetion*, meaning the middle sanctuary was located in Scotland. Researchers speculate that all of these places were once holy or sacred places to the Celtic people.

Celtic mythology is also full of references to sacred groves and holy trees. Heroes and characters in Celtic legends, such as Mac Cuill (son of Hazel) and Mac Ibar (son of Yew) have tree names, and a mysterious being called Man in the Tree appears in some legends. The strength of the Celtic myths, according to historian Ross, is evidence of a belief in the sacredness of trees and groves. She says, "trees and woods . . . [were] amongst the most important of the sacred precincts of the Celts, whether or not they were distinguished by any more sophisticated associated structure."[60]

Gods and Goddesses of the Celts

It was in these sacred places, the waterways and the mighty tree groves, that the Celts worshipped their gods and goddesses. These deities played a vital role in Celtic civilization. Not only were they a source of power to be revered, but they were also a link between the everyday lives of the Celts and the mysterious powers of the natural world. Ross explains this, saying, "The everyday life of the Celts included the supernatural equally with the natural, the divine with the mundane; for them the Otherworld was as real as the tangible world and as ever-present."[61]

The names of more than four hundred Celtic gods and goddesses have been recorded by historians. Many of them were local gods, worshipped by individual tribes in specific locations. Little is known about these gods other than their names. Some, however, were clearly major gods that were probably worshipped by the entire Celtic civilization. These powerful gods appear in myths and inscriptions, and place-names derived from their names can be found throughout the Celtic world.

Celtic Goddesses

Celtic goddesses were powerful female deities. They were concerned with the fertility of crops, livestock, and with the well-being of Celtic people themselves. Some were mighty war-goddesses who had magical powers on the battlefield. However, the most revered female deities were the mother-goddesses. The Celts viewed the mother-goddesses as part of the life-giving forces of the earth. According to Green,

> The divine fertility-element in Celtic society is . . . clearly seen in the various types of Mother-Goddesses. . . . Images of a goddess associated with life and abundance are physical manifestations of a community endeavoring to control the behavior of the seasons and to appease . . . the forces who imposed the cycle of life and death.[62]

One of the greatest mother-goddesses was Danu, whose name means divine waters from heaven. An Irish Celtic creation myth tells that Danu created the Danuvius (Danube) river, from which the Tuatha de Danann (Children of Danu) sprang. The Children of Danu were a race of gods, including deities of learning, magical skills, arts, and crafts. Rivers throughout Europe,

THE MORRIGAN: GODDESSES OF BATTLE AND DEATH

No Celtic deities were more frightening than the trio of war-goddesses known collectively as the Morrigan. They were the goddesses of war, death, and destruction. Their power can be seen in the many stories and legends that tell of their exploits.

The Morrigan appear under different names throughout Celtic mythology. Morrigan is the name of one goddess and also the name of the group. The other goddesses sometimes included in the Morrigan were Badb, Macha, and Nemain. The Badb is also sometimes known as Badb Catha, the Battle Raven.

The appearance of these goddesses on the field of battle could strike terror into any Celt who saw them. One moment they would be hideous hags; the next they would transform into beautiful maidens. They might fly to the battlefield in the form of black ravens, feeding on the flesh of the dead.

These war-goddesses were the epitome of strength, power, and sexual energy. They represented the magical—and fearsome—aspect of war and death.

including the Danube in Germany, have been named for Danu, indicating her importance to the Celtic world.

Likewise, the *Deae Matres*, or triple mothers, were a group of three goddesses who represented the earth and fertility. They carried symbols of the life-giving earth such as baskets of fruit, loaves of bread, and children. There is no record that these goddesses had individual names; they were simply referred to as the mothers, and they appear to have been worshipped as such throughout Celtic Europe.

Brigit was another powerful Celtic goddess. She was the daughter of Dagda, the greatest Celtic god. The Celts worshipped her as the patron of poets and the goddess of healing. She was known as Brigantia in Northern Britain, an area still referred to as Brigantia. One of the four major Celtic holidays, Imbolc, celebrated on February 1, is associated with her.

Epona was the Celtic horse goddess. The importance of horses in Celtic society can be seen in the hundreds of statues and carvings depicting Epona that archaeologists have unearthed. Although nothing is known of the specific ways that the Celts worshipped Epona, researchers suspect that her power was pervasive, for the Romans mentioned her a great deal. They also adopted her as one of their own goddesses.

Celtic Gods

The Celtic gods were no less powerful than their female counterparts. The greatest male Celtic deity was Dagda, whose name means the good god. He was not good in a moral sense, but was skilled at everything. Legend portrays Dadga as a powerful warrior who was considered to be the father of the gods in Irish Celtic mythology. He carried a gigantic club with magical powers: one end could kill; the other end could heal. The club was so massive that he had to drag it behind him on wheels.

He also possessed a gigantic cauldron, known as the cauldron of plenty, that provided food so no one would ever go hungry. Archaeologists have found many cauldrons, which are different from ordinary cooking utensils. Some of them are beautifully decorated, while others sometimes contain objects such as weapons. This suggests to archaeologists that cauldrons were very important to Celtic worship and religious beliefs.

The god Lugh is believed by some to be even greater than Dagda. This is suggested by the dozens of place-names in Europe that are linked to Lugh, as Ellis says, "The name appears in place-names in many of the former Celtic territories: Lyons, Leon, Loudan and Laon in France; Leiden in Holland; Liegnitz in Silesia, and Carlisle (Luguvalum in Roman times) in England. It has been argued that the name of London . . . also derived from Lugdunum."[63]

Little is known about how the Celts worshipped Lugh, but one of the major Celtic holidays was Lughnasad, or Lugnasa. This holiday began on August 1 and lasted for one month. Traces of it still survive in some parts of Britain and Ireland.

Another powerful Celtic god was Cernunnos, whose name means the horned one. He is usually depicted as having the antlers of a stag. He was the Celtic god of fertility, animals, and wealth. Little is known about the specific beliefs surrounding Cernunnos, but a great number of Celtic artifacts and artworks depict horned figures, suggesting that he was widely worshipped. The fact that Cernunnos was associated with the stag, an animal very important to the Celts, gives credence to the idea that the Celts believed this god was powerful.

These gods and hundreds of others filled the Celtic world. They cared for the land and the people, and in return the Celts worshipped them. But each tribe had its own local gods as well, and it was up to the druids, the intellectual class of thinkers and priests, to make sense of the dizzying number of gods and the beliefs associated with them. As Green relates, "The druids, in matters of ritual at least, may have had a unifying role."[64]

The Druids

Many ancient writers talk about the Celtic druids, describing their rituals and their beliefs within the Celtic civilization. However, very little is really known or understood about this group of Celtic intellectuals. The biggest problem with understanding the role of the druids in Celtic society is that they did not leave any written records of their beliefs or rituals. Because the druids did not believe in recording their knowlege in their own language, historians must use other sources to discover information about them.

The main sources of information about the druids are the works of classical writers (the Romans especially), and this information is sketchy at best. The Romans were the Celts' biggest enemy, and Roman writers tended to discuss the Celts in very negative terms. Many of the descriptions left by Roman writers are biased, propaganda meant to discredit the Celts and the druids. Few other records of the druids have survived.

Druids in religious costume. The druids were part of one of the highest classses of Celts.

As a result, there are many things that historians do not know about the druids. It is not known if they were common in tribes throughout the Celtic world, whether they were important priests or merely intellectual teachers, or even whether they rose and fell in popularity during specific times in Celtic history. All researchers know for certain, according to Ross, is that, "At some period in their history some of the Celtic peoples had powerful priests of this name, who kept the often hostile forces of the Otherworld at bay, and knew the correct ritual which could canalize [call on] these [their own] powers for the good and benefit of mankind in general and the tribe in particular."[65]

With this idea in mind, modern scholars have pieced together information from

records and references from ancient historians and have come up with some information about the druids. They believe that throughout the Celtic civilization, the druids served as leaders, conducted rituals, and studied science and nature. Their position in Celtic society, one of the highest classes of citizens, attests to the fact that the druids were indeed some of the most important Celts in their culture.

Druids as Intellectual Leaders

Druids were considered to be part of the most respected intellectual order in Celtic civilization. Not only were they priests, but they were also a group or class of men called *druides* that included judges, teachers, historians, poets, musicians, philosophers, physicians, astronomers, and political counselors. Some druids became kings or chieftains of certain Celtic tribes.

Training to become a druid leader was long and difficult. The only information about druid training that has survived is from Ireland, but scholars speculate that it may have been similar for other groups. For the Irish Celts, this training involved study that lasted for many years, as students laboriously committed all knowledge to memory. Most druids began their training by becoming bards, who memorized the history and stories of the civilization and then retold the stories. According to historian Christiane Eluere,

> [The druid's] initiation included several intermediate stages. Thus, the course of study for an Irish bard included verse forms, composition and recitation of tales, the study of grammar, *ogham* [a Celtic form of writing], philosophy and law. The next seven

51

years were for more specialist studies and included the secret language of the poets. . . . He could then acquire the knowledge of genealogy, and the committal of events and laws into poetic form to become a doctor of law. Finally the "man of learning" would be fit to study incantations, divination [seeing the future] and magical practice.[66]

Once a druid had completed his training, he was qualified to take on his role as leader within the tribe. In many cases, this included serving as a judge to settle disputes. The Celts did not have an organized judicial system, but used their druids as judges. At certain times of the year, according to Caesar, druids gathered at a sacred place in Gaul to sit in judgment after a crime, such as robbery or murder, occurred. Celts traveled to this place to have their cases heard and judged by the druids. Although nothing is known about how they reached their decisions, it is clear that the druids' decisions were final. According to Caesar,

> They hand out compensations and penalties. If some individual . . . refuses to accept their decision they ban him from sacrifices: This is the most exquisite penalty among them. People who incur this ban are relegated to the ranks of the impious and criminals; everyone shuns them. . . . They are refused all access to justice and have no share in any honor.[67]

Another important function of the druids in Celtic society was that of historian. Many of the Irish Celtic myths and legends are be-lieved to relate actual historical events that were committed to memory as stories and poems centuries before. For example, an Irish work called *The Book of Invasions* is a medieval document that relates the mythological history of Ireland. It includes many characters from ancient mythology, and historians suspect that some of the events in the book might have actually occurred. These stories were likely passed down from ancient Celtic druids.

Roman writers also mention druids' historical knowledge. In A.D. 69, for example, the Roman writer Tacitus related that the druid historians of Gaul knew that the Celts had defeated the Roman army and sacked Rome more than three hundred years before. Clearly, these important historical events had been memorized and passed down for more than three centuries, indicating the vital importance of history to the druids and to the Celtic civilization as a whole.

Druids as Religious Leaders

The druids were also in control of the religious and spiritual functions of the tribe. Very little is known about the specific religious rituals of the Celts, but a few written sources hint at what some of them might have been. The fact that the Celts revered water, for example, suggests that they had some water-purification rituals. Early Irish sources speak of one ritual, somewhat like a baptism, that druids performed. It is unclear whether this ritual was purely Celtic or if it was introduced to the Celts by Christians.

Additionally, druids had funeral rituals for the dead. The Celts believed that a deceased person would be reborn in the Otherworld, so there were special rituals and celebrations to mark the occasion. The body was washed and wrapped, then it was watched for a number of days. After this watching period, or wake, the druids chanted and spoke over the body, which was then covered with leafy birch branches and carried to the grave.

There are also scattered mentions of the Celts performing ritual sacrifices in the presence of their druids. Ancient writers mentioned sacrifices, such as this example from the historian Strabo, "They [the Celts] used to strike a man, whom they had devoted to death, in the back with a knife, and then divine [predict the future] from his death-throes; but they did not sacrifice without a Druid."[68]

Strabo also talked of the Celts building a huge structure of straw and wood, throwing cattle and humans inside, and burning it. Many historians dismiss these horrific accounts of human sacrifice as Roman attempts to discredit the Celtic civilization. Although it is possible that druids practiced human sacrifice, little evidence remains to prove it.

When Christianity supplanted the Celtic religions in the first centuries of the first mil-

The Whickerman, a huge structure of straw and wood in which, according to Strabo, people and animals were burnt as sacrifices to Celtic gods. Some historians, however, dismiss these accounts of human sacrifice as Roman propoganda.

lennium A.D., the role of druids in Celtic society decreased. Many druids embraced the new teachings of Christianity and adjusted their knowledge to their new beliefs. Slowly, the ancient knowledge and stories disappeared, and the druids and the Celtic religion were forgotten.

CHAPTER FIVE

THE GOLDEN AGE OF CELTIC ART

For centuries, few people realized that the Celtic civilization had given birth to one of the most extraordinary art styles that has ever been created. Few examples of their artwork survived, and the artifacts that were found were scattered throughout the world. There were some tantalizing clues to the Celts' extraordinary artistic style, however. Ancient illuminated manuscripts in European monasteries and museums, a few pieces of jewelry, some examples of statuary, and other artifacts were covered with ornate decorations. This style, based on elements in the natural world, was filled with vines, animals, and geometric figures of flowing lines and brilliant colors.

The rise and flowering of Celtic art followed the civilization's evolution to prominence in Europe. As the Celtic society spread throughout the ancient world, it grew powerful and confident. Its art mirrored that confidence, revealing a strong culture that was capable of creating exquisite beauty. In the words of historians Dillon and Chadwick, "From the earliest times until its last fine flowering . . . Celtic art is a rich and highly individual development. . . . It is distinguished by a fundamental individuality which is essentially Celtic, and which re-

mains constant throughout history wherever the Celtic peoples are found."[69]

The Rise of Celtic Art

Historians have described Celtic art as the first great contribution by the barbarians to European art. They speculate that the Celts created artworks from the earliest days of their history, but there is little evidence to confirm this. No one knows when or how Celtic artisans developed their techniques and styles. But they created a sophisticated and highly skilled style that was breathtaking—and completely original.

It is this originality and its obvious celebration of the natural world that distinguishes Celtic art from any other art form. As Dillon and Chadwick relate, "Perhaps the most fundamental [quality] is its originality, the choice and combination of the motifs, chiefly from the world of nature, the animal and vegetable world . . . the whole forming a fantastic creation of the imagination, removed from reality."[70]

This originality baffles historians. The Celts, a warlike, supposedly barbarian culture, seemed to create a new style of art completely out of the blue. But the Celts lived in a world populated by many other cultures, and it is possible that early Celtic artisans were inspired by other cultures including the Romans, Greeks, Etruscans, and the Egyptians. Each had its own artistic style, all of which were well established by the time the first Celtic tribes are mentioned in the sixth century B.C. Many historians speculate that the Celts borrowed some artistic ideas from them.

When the Celts began importing Greek wines, for example, the wine was stored in jugs decorated with typical Greek motifs such as twining vines and plants. Some historians speculate that these motifs, combined with other art styles and the Celts' own creative style, could have been the inspiration for the early development of Celtic art. As Ross explains,

> By combining these Classical [Greek] patterns with the old indigenous artist and religious motifs of Bronze Age Europe—the sacred water-birds, the solar symbols and so on—with . . . geometric forms, and with the splendid animal art of the Persians and Scythians [ancient cultures] and more Easterly peoples, they evolved this entirely new, original, and exciting art style.[71]

Regardless of the inspiration, Celtic artisans were definitely creating original art during the Hallstatt period, a time of great change in the Celtic world. Tribes were spilling out of the north and settling throughout Europe. People had discovered the amazing power of iron and had begun using it for their weapons and agriculture. Some Celtic villages grew wealthy from trade with the rest of the world. And the belief in the power of the natural world pervaded the entire society.

Many of the motifs they used in their art were inspired by the swirling chaos of plant and animal life around them. As Delaney explains,

> The deepest basis of Celtic art grew from a primordial dependence upon the natural life experienced in the emergent Europe. . . . The early motifs showed great consistency of pattern, geometric, singular shapes, concentric circles, whorls, lozenges, revolving spirals, chevrons, [and] cross-hatched repeating patterns. Later, the images of small creatures begin to materialise, swans, ducks, horses . . . a goat, a sphinx, a lion, a deer.[72]

One of the most famous examples of Hallstatt Celtic art is a case, called a scabbard, that holds a sword. It is decorated with a series of men, perhaps soldiers, carrying shields and spears. Some are on horseback, while others march on foot. Celtic playfulness and originality shine from the faces of each soldier. Delaney describes the scabbard as "decorated concisely with figures of men with recognizable personalities, small, almost comic, engaged in wrestling . . . discussing a spoked wheel, marching on foot, carrying decorated shields, charging on horseback, helmeted, with their horses trampling enemies."[73]

La Tène Art

As the Celtic civilization flourished, the exquisite beauty and originality of its art continued to develop. The geometric motifs of the Hallstatt period gave way to more complex designs. Flowing lines, details, and ornamentation became more intricate. By the beginning of the La Tène period, Celtic art

GUNDESTRUP CAULDRON

Magic cauldrons often appear in Celtic legend and myth. The cauldron was a symbol of rebirth to the Celts; the dead were put in and returned alive. Many cauldrons have been found at Celtic archeological sites. One of the most beautiful examples is the Gundestrup Cauldron. This large bowl is not only a magnificent example of Celtic art, but it is also an object that probably played a vital role in Celtic religious beliefs.

Found in Denmark, it was made sometime during the first century B.C. It is a silver-plated copper bowl covered with beautiful Celtic motifs in high relief. The images of many gods cover the outside of the cauldron, and mythological scenes fill the inside. The antler-headed god Cernunnos sits cross-legged, surrounded by animals, in one scene. In another, a god holds a dead warrior over a cauldron while previously dead soldiers march away, reinforcing the Celtic idea that the cauldron was a symbol of rebirth. Other lively images include all manner of animals, birds, and human masks. Each scene had some kind of meaning to the Celts, whether it was an image of a god, an animal, or a ritual. When the Gundestrup Cauldron was found, it had been deliberately taken apart and carefully laid on the ground, as an offering—one that would have certainly pleased the god to whom it was given.

The Gundestrup Cauldron is one of the finest examples of Celtic craftsmenship still in existance today.

had evolved into the breathtaking style that it is known for today.

The La Tène period is the true golden age of Celtic art. The style had become refined and sophisticated, but it was still completely original. Artists let their imaginations run away with them to create what Dillon and Chadwick describe as,

> fantastic combinations of animals and foliage, bizarre and unnatural images of natural objects, the flora and fauna of the East [such as Egypt and Asia], lotuses, palms, lions, and the wild beasts of the desert, divorced from their realistic images and recombined in alien settings. . . . It is the art of a people intensely aware of their environment in the world of nature.[74]

Most of the Celtic artwork from the La Tène period consists of domestic and personal art. The Celts loved jewelry, for example, and they wore great amounts of gold, beads, and amber. Many thick, twisted, golden neck torques filled with Celtic motifs from this period have been discovered. The heads of animals, some realistic, some fantastic, decorate the terminals, or ends of the torques. Exquisite brooches and pins are swirled with enameled designs in deep reds, blues, greens, and golds. Colorful glass beads and bangles indicate that the Celts were skilled at glassmaking.

As archaeologists have discovered, nature surges through La Tène art. The Celts' belief in the power of nature appears in the thousands of detailed designs that have survived. From the grandest jewelry and weaponry to the smallest details on tiny glass beads, Celtic art is indeed the art of the natural world.

The Celts loved jewelry (like this inlaid bronze brooch) and wore a lot of gold, beads, and amber.

Animals in Celtic Art

The La Tène artifacts are filled with representations of all kinds of wild and domesticated animals. These display a creative and original mix of real and fantastic elements. Many of the animals in Celtic art were the creatures that the people knew well, such as swans, ducks, horses, goats, and deer. These were created to look lifelike, but they were embellished with curls and flowing lines that gave them a supernatural feel.

Celtic artisans of the La Tène period had the ability to make animals come to life in their art. Even though many of the animals had intricate, abstract details, the Celts managed to convey the animals' personality in delightful ways.

CELTIC JEWELRY: MAGNIFICENT BROOCHES

The Celts loved to wear beautiful jewelry, and many contemporary descriptions tell of them wearing golden neck rings (called torques), bracelets, arm bands, and other adornments. Their love of beauty and color is nowhere more apparent than in two remarkable Celtic brooches.

The Hunterston brooch, found in Scotland, is a little less than five inches around. It is filled with interlacing animal images, Celtic spirals, and trumpet patterns made of gold and silver set with stones of amber.

Even more impressive, however, is the Tara brooch from Ireland. This brooch is considered to be one of the most precious items in Ireland. It is made of a ring of molded bronze, and its surface is divided into small spaces that are filled with Celtic swirls, whorls, circles, and geometric designs. Animal heads stretch out of some of the areas. The entire brooch is decorated with red enamel, amber, small disks of blue and red glass, and tiny human heads carved in amethyst.

These two brooches are unique, but they display a refined skill that was a hallmark of Celtic artistry. They are extraordinary examples of the beauty with which the Celts filled their world.

One of the most famous examples, called the Basse-Yutz flagons, are wonderful examples of the Celts' love of animals. These bronze flagons, or large pitchers, were probably used to serve wine and were made in about the fourth century B.C. The long, elegant spouts are decorated with swirls and geometric patterns in the Celtic style. At the top of the spout sits a small duck with bright eyes made of coral. Little does it know that behind it, making up the lid and handle of the flagon, are three ferocious beasts crouched quietly, watching. The largest, a doglike creature, holds the lid chain tightly in its mouth.

The entire scene captures the essence of animals in nature: the unsuspecting duck, the hunting beasts. The details show the enormous skill of the Celtic craftsman who made it and his obvious understanding of animal behavior. Historian Delaney says, "The Basse-Yutz flagons communicate several facts central to Celtic art. . . . A spirit of decoration which did not fear to reach for playful shapes—in turn derived from natural, animal, or vegetal forms, heading in the direction of the unreal or the surreal, inventive, abstract."[75]

These flagons are so exquisite that historians suspect they probably graced the table of a wealthy Celtic chieftain. Wine, an imported drink, was expensive. Only the highest members of Celtic society probably drank it, so it makes sense that the flagons used to serve it would be equally rich.

Human Figures in Celtic Art

Although artisans of the Celtic civilization seemed to prefer using motifs from nature, human figures appear as well, albeit less often, and they are usually shown along with animal and other natural motifs. This mix of human and animal images can be seen throughout Celtic art, from the earliest examples of the Hallstatt period to the stunning illuminated manuscripts of the Celtic Christian era in the first centuries of the first millenium A.D. As Chadwick relates, "There is, for example, a . . . keen awareness on the part of the artists of the plant and animal life around them. With these the human head is sometimes curiously blended. Sometimes a mask, animal or human, appears . . . amidst the foliage."[76]

Celtic artisans also depicted human forms in sculptures and jewelry. Many miniature human figures, busts, and heads have been discovered throughout Europe. Dillon and Chadwick describe one bronze relief that was probably made during the fourth century B.C., an example of a typical human form in Celtic art, with "prominent eyes, triangular nose, the emphasized eyebrows, the narrow slit mouth, absence of clearly marked ears, a framework of two leaves pointing downwards, and an upturned curl at the tip, which may well have developed as a stylized form of hair."[77]

The Importance of the Head

The Celts incorporated human heads a great deal in their art. They believed that the head contained the soul of a person, and Celtic warriors were known for decapitating their enemies in battle and keeping the heads. Historians contend that the frequent depiction of heads in Celtic art harked back to this belief. The Celts decorated jewelry, weapons, household objects, and later, illuminated manuscripts with images of human heads; even flagon handles were decorated with skillfully rendered heads. Shields carried images of heads that seemed to stare out at their enemies. Heads were worked into the designs of golden torques. Ross describes one such torque: "Human heads are worked into the spiral design and the spirals emerging from the brow and continuing up the side of the head look as though they are intended to represent horns."[78]

Heads are also depicted on Celtic stone sculpture. One two-headed sculpture, found in Germany, is one and a half times life size. It has all the characteristics of Celtic human imagery, including straight eyebrows, a slit-like mouth and a triangular nose. Little more is known about this sculpture.

The Celts also made many human-head masks throughout all periods of the Celtic civilization. Although the masks were hollow, historians believe these were not supposed to be worn. Instead, they may have been used as some sort of religious symbol, either inserted on a pillar or displayed on an altar. Chadwick describes one such mask, "A mask of a Celtic hero from the Pyrenees [mountains along the border of France and Spain] is incised [etched] on a bronze sheet and is open at the back . . . with holes cut out for the eyes, which are absent, but were made of enamel or stones; the whole was originally fixed on a wooden pillar."[79]

The Entire Human Form

Not only did the Celts use human-head imagery in their sculptures, but they also depicted the entire human form. Archaeologists have found numerous Celtic human figure sculptures in the area of Celtic Gaul, now modern-day France and Belgium, near the mouth of the Rhone river. Some of the statuary was life-sized and was carved wearing Celtic clothing and armor. These statues most likely depicted the tribal heroes, kings, and queens of a Gaulish Celtic tribe, although historians do not know this for certain.

The Celts created another type of human figure sculpture, that of small carvings called votive offerings. They cast these carvings into sacred waters as offerings to the goddess of that particular area or as a plea for healing from the gods of a particular body part. Many such carvings have been found in a sanctuary known as Sequana at the source of the Seine River in France, a very sacred place to Celts. Dillon and Chadwick describe the amazing array of statuary that archaeologists found at the site,

> This initial find produced 27 statues or statuettes of half a metre to 1.25 metres in height; 40 heads from life to half-life size; 16 pieces with 2 or 3 heads carved in relief on a single stave [stick]; 14 torsos. . . . About 30 limbs and some representations of the human internal organs. . . . Men and women were both represented, and . . . travellers (perhaps pilgrims) recognizable by their cloaks and hoods.[80]

These votive offerings depicting the human form were just one way that the Celts

The Celts often incorporated human heads in their art because they believed that the head contained a person's soul.

incorporated human imagery into their art. Humans were, to the Celtic culture, an integral part of the natural world. People constantly interacted with nature and the gods, either symbolically through their religious beliefs or in reality through their daily lives of hunting and farming. In their artwork, Celtic artisans celebrated this link between the Celtic people and their religious beliefs.

Art, Myth, and Religion

The Celts filled their lives with art that depicted their spiritual beliefs. Animals that represented strength appeared on Celtic weapons. Images of gods and goddesses graced the sacred places where the Celts worshipped. Objects were decorated with combinations of animal and human pictures that told stories of the gods or legends from the Celts' heroic past. Their art, according to Ross, represents the spirit of the Celtic civilization, its beliefs, and its people,

> In their art style, then, we come very close to the essence of the Celtic temperament. It reflects the tortuous and subtle nature of their thought processes; the complexities of their language: it makes manifest the complicated, shifting, oblique nature of their religious attitudes. In short, Celtic art is an impressive summing up of all that is fundamental and distinctive in the spiritual life of the Celts.[81]

One of the most original and beautiful examples of the Celtic ability to mix religion, myth, and daily life in their artwork is a small metal wagon from the Hallstatt period. The wagon, made of bronze, is filled with standing human figures. In the center, a goddess stands tall, holding a bowl above her head. The bowl may have been used as an incense burner. She is surrounded by horsemen and soldiers carrying spears and shields. On either end of the wagon, warriors grasp stags by their antlers.

This beautiful wagon brings together many images that were sacred to the Celts. The stag, for example, represented the spirit of the forest, and the Celts admired the animal's agility and speed. One of their powerful gods, Cernunnos, was a stag-horned god. The wagon might represent a ritual stag hunt, or it could be a symbol of the strength in battle.

Another way that the Celts expressed their beliefs through their art was in their coins. In the late third century B.C., the Celts began making and using their own coinage, and artisans decorated the coins with a variety of motifs from their beliefs. As Ross explains, "The coins . . . are potentially a repository for mythological tradition, as well as being a stimulating and challenging medium for the display of the Celtic artists."[82]

It is unclear exactly which myths and stories the coins depict, but they show a dizzying array of images and designs both from the Celtic spiritual system and the natural world. Some show severed heads, while others have a puzzling image of the legs of horses that have become detached from their bodies. Many show various animals and birds that have religious significance. Celtic artisans let their imaginations go, and the result was a beautiful mix of religious and natural motifs.

Another object, found in France, also shows this creative mix of religion and legend. The bronze object is decorated with a running spiral design with three human heads. Many

CELTIC GODS OF METALWORKERS

In the Celtic civilization, artistry was highly respected. Smiths who worked with metals enjoyed high status within the tribe and were considered to be part of the intellectual class. Some historians suspect that this was because metalworkers and artisans were believed to possess some magical powers, the ability to make beautiful and useful objects from rough raw ore.

The Celts even had a specific god of smiths. In some legends, he is called Goibhniu, and he was one of three gods who controlled all metalworking. The other two gods were named Luchta and Creidhne. According to legend, they worked together to produce weapons, jewelry, and other metal objects.

Celtic gods appeared in groups of three, so the appearance of three heads could signify some specific ritual significance. The heads, however, were crafted with strange, distorted features. One eye was huge while the other was small; the hair was streaked back on one side and left loose on the other; beards grew on only one side of the face.

Due to the specific disfigurements on the heads of this object, historian Ross suggests that these heads might represent a part of the story of the famous Celtic hero Cu Chulainn: "Then his face became a red hollow [hole]. He sucked one of his eyes into his head so that a wild crane could hardly have reached it to pluck it out from the back of his skull on to the middle of his cheek. The other eye sprang out on to his cheek. His mouth was twisted back fearsomely."[83]

Celtic art reached its peak in the last centuries before the fall of the civilization. During that time, the Celts created some of the most breathtaking art in the world. Then, with the Roman conquest and the advent of Christianity, Celtic art declined. Ireland, however, was the last part of the Celtic world to fall, and it continued the Celtic art tradition for centuries after it had disappeared in the rest of Europe. But slowly, it too disappeared. For centuries, much of the art lay buried, hidden beneath sacred waters and the rich graves of Celtic princes. It has been only in the last century that archaeologists have unearthed these exquisite examples of Celtic art. These pieces show that the Celtic civilization, once thought of by the Romans as having no art, was one of the most artistic cultures the world has ever seen.

CHAPTER SIX

WARFARE AND BLOOD

Warfare played a vital role in Celtic civilization. Although the Celts built a stable, agricultural system, their society was founded on conquest. From the earliest days of Celtic history, tribes migrated and fought their way through Europe, eventually settling in areas from the Po valley in Italy to the far reaches of Ireland. Along the way, they battled the various cultures they met for land and wealth.

Many ancient writers who described the Celts and their penchant for warfare believed that the civilization conducted war simply for the sake of fighting. According to Strabo,

> The whole race, which is now called Celtic or Galatic, is madly fond of war, high-spirited and quick to battle, but otherwise straightforward and not of evil character. . . . For at any time or place, and on whatever pretext you stir them up, you will have them ready to face danger, even if they have nothing on their side but their own strength and courage.[84]

To the Celts, war was normal and desirable, but they did not wage war simply for the sport of it. Celtic warfare was a means by which a warrior proved his strength and prowess and established status within the tribe. Celtic soldiers who proved themselves in battle were part of the highest social class

in Celtic society. Warfare was, therefore, the predominant way for the Celtic civilization to choose and honor its leaders. It was also the way the Celts acquired material wealth. Raids, for example, played a significant role in Celtic society. During a raid, a band of Celtic warriors might attack a neighboring tribe, stealing their cattle and other goods. Raids could be small, conducted against a neighboring Celtic settlement. They could be large, with tribes sometimes even banding together temporarily to attack bigger areas. Ocassionally, raids would become full-scale battles in which tribes fought for land and slaves. Raids provided tribes with land, cattle, and other material wealth. They were also an opportunity for soldiers to gain glory in battle.

Rules of Warfare

The Celts followed specific rules of warfare that reflected the attitudes of honor and respect within their society. High among their rules was the concept of single combat. Since glory was achieved through individual courage, individuals had to prove themselves. One of the most important rules of single combat was what the Irish called *fir fer* or fair play. Under this rule, if a warrior offered single combat, he would be opposed by only one person from the enemy side. In many cases, two leaders might meet one-on-one on the field, with their armies behind them. The

Warfare in Celtic society was a way for men to prove their strength and establish status within the tribe.

outcome of this single battle could decide the entire war. Anyone who broke these rules would cast great shame and dishonor onto himself and his entire tribe.

Much of the Celtic idea of honorable battle and its importance can be seen in their religion and in their stories. The Celts believed that their tribal gods were excellent warriors and that they played an active role in warfare. The gods might appear and fight alongside them, for example, or a great godlike Celtic king might do battle for a god in some otherworldly fight, a fight that includes gods or was held in a supernatural place. As Ross says, "The semi-divine hero may stand in for the god in single combat; the god could come and aid the semi-divine hero in a similar situation. The weapons of the great heroes were alleged to be inhabited or motivated by the gods."[85]

Many Celtic legends tell the stories of great warriors who gain glory in battle. One legend, for example, relates an incident in the childhood of Cu Chulainn, a famous Celtic hero.

One day, a druid named Cathbad was teaching his students when one of them asked if he saw a special omen for the day. Cathbad replied that a boy who should take up arms on that day would be famous but would be short-lived. Cu Chulainn heard this and immediately went to his uncle Conchobar, who was king and asked to be given weapons. When the king demanded an explanation, the boy told him of his teacher's prophecy. Then the young Cu Chulainn said, "It is a wonderful thing, if I am but one day and one night in the world, provided that my fame and my deeds live after me."[86]

Cu Chulainn went on to become one of the most legendary Celtic heroes. His story illustrates the warrior spirit that honored glory in battle above all else. This spirit and importance of warriors affected the entire society.

Celtic Warriors and Society

Celtic warriors held the most honorable positions in the Celtic civilization, and they were considered to be part of the highest class of society. Caesar called them knights and wrote of them, saying, "These, when there is occasion and when any war occurs . . . are all engaged in war. And those of them most distinguished by birth and resources, have the greatest number of vassals [soldiers] and dependents about them. They acknowledge this sort of influence and power only."[87]

Caesar was correct in saying that many of the Celtic leaders were influential; they had many followers, and they were often wealthy.

Each tribe usually had a powerful leader as well as a number of warriors who followed him. This group of soldiers was sometimes called a *comitatus* and was large or small, depending on how powerful a leader was and how many men would follow him into battle.

A Celtic chieftain was expected to lead his warriors into battle often. He was also expected to be the best fighter in the tribe. It was a dishonor for his troops to surpass him in skill or valor, but it was also dishonorable if the warriors failed to equal their leader in battle. This created a balance by which every Celtic soldier was expected to do his best while honoring the leadership of his king.

Warfare provided a way for Celtic soldiers to achieve personal glory and honor, two of the most important aspects of Celtic society.

Victory in battle brought fame and wealth, which benefitted the entire tribe. A successful raiding campaign, for example, could result in vast new riches including gold, jewelry, and cattle. After a raid, the chieftain usually divided the booty among his soldiers as a reward for their service. Victory against a particular foe, such as a rival chieftain or a foreign invader, brought even more glory. Warfare also allowed the chieftain to strengthen the bonds of loyalty between himself and his soldiers by sharing the dangers and successes of the battlefield.

In return, a Celtic warrior was expected to give his lord his full support in whatever the leader thought was important. It was his responsibility to fight fiercely and honorably for his chieftain. Celtic warriors fought beside their lord; they protected

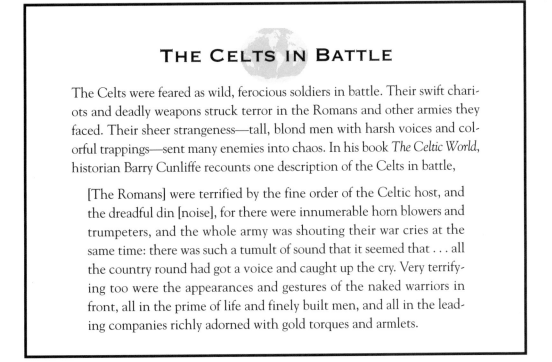

THE CELTS IN BATTLE

The Celts were feared as wild, ferocious soldiers in battle. Their swift chariots and deadly weapons struck terror in the Romans and other armies they faced. Their sheer strangeness—tall, blond men with harsh voices and colorful trappings—sent many enemies into chaos. In his book *The Celtic World*, historian Barry Cunliffe recounts one description of the Celts in battle,

> [The Romans] were terrified by the fine order of the Celtic host, and the dreadful din [noise], for there were innumerable horn blowers and trumpeters, and the whole army was shouting their war cries at the same time: there was such a tumult of sound that it seemed that . . . all the country round had got a voice and caught up the cry. Very terrifying too were the appearances and gestures of the naked warriors in front, all in the prime of life and finely built men, and all in the leading companies richly adorned with gold torques and armlets.

A Celtic chieftan, was expected to lead his warriors into battle and be the best fighter in the tribe.

him during battle; and if the chieftain died, they avenged his death.

The Gaesatae

Within the warrior class of the Celts were elite warrior bands. Although little is known about these bands except their names, the fact that their names do survive indicates that they achieved greatness through battle and victory. Irish sources mention many of them, including the Craobh Ruadh (Red Branch) warriors of Ulster and the Degad, a band of warriors that was exiled to Munster.

One of the best known warrior bands was a group of soldiers known as the Gaesatae. They were fierce Celtic warriors who charged into battle naked. Ancient writers such as Polybius mention the Gaesatae, saying,

The Gaesatae had been moved by their thirst for glory and their defiant spirit to throw away [their] garments and so they took up their positions in front of the whole army naked and wearing nothing but their arms [weapons]. They believed that they would be better equipped for action in this state, as the ground was in places overgrown with brambles and these might catch in their clothes and hamper them in the use of their weapons.[88]

For centuries, this description was interpreted by some to suggest that all Celtic warriors fought naked, but this was not the case. The Gaesatae were unique. In fact they were not a Celtic tribe, as the ancient writers thought. Instead, they were an elite band of professional warriors who fought nude because of their religious beliefs. They believed that fighting naked intensified their luck and power in battle and, as Ellis says, "This contact with Mother Earth added to their spiritual aura, ensuring rebirth in the Otherworld if they perished in this one."[89]

Weaponry

The Gaesatae, as well as other Celtic warriors, relied on more than luck in battle, however. They were equipped with some of the most effective weapons in the world at that time. Their swords, armor, and battle chariots struck fear in their enemies and helped the Celts become the most feared civilization in the world.

This fear is seen in an account by the ancient writer Plutarch. After a battle in which a Roman army was defeated by the Celts, a Roman commander realized that the Celts had defeated him with superior weapons and tactics. As a result, says Plutarch, the commander decided to equip his own soldiers with new weapons, just like the Celts used.

> Knowing the prowess of the Barbarians lay chiefly in their swords, which they plied in true barbaric fashion . . . he [the Roman commander] had helmets forged for most of his men which were all iron and smooth of surface, that the enemy's swords might slip off from them or be shattered by them. He also had the long shields of his men rimmed round with bronze, since their wood could not of itself ward off the enemy's blows.[90]

Many other ancient writers commented on the superiority of Celtic weaponry. Since few examples of Celtic weapons have survived, historians rely on such accounts to give a

A Roman legionaire (left) and a Celtic warrior (right) as depicted on the Column of Antoninus, in Rome. Celtic soldiers often proved to be fierce opponents.

clearer picture of what types of weapons the Celts used. The ancient Roman writer Siculus Didodorus says,

> Their armor includes man-sized shields decorated in individual fashion. Some of these have projecting bronze animals of fine workmanship which serve for defence as well as decoration. On their heads they wear bronze helmets which possess large projecting figures lending the appearance of enormous stature to the wearer. In some cases horns form one piece with the helmet while in other cases it is relief figures of the foreparts of birds or quadrupeds. . . . Instead of the short sword they carry long swords held by iron or bronze chains and hanging along their right flank. . . . Their spears which they brandish in battle, and which they call *lanciae*, have iron heads a cubit or more in length and a little less than two palms in breadth; for their swords are as long as the javelins of other peoples, and their javelins have points longer than their swords.[91]

In the early days of the Celtic civilization, swords were made of bronze. During the Hallstatt period, however, the Celts adopted iron and began to build the deadly iron swords they became known for. Iron made a significant difference in the quality of Celtic weapons and their effectiveness in battle.

The first swords were short, cut-and-thrust weapons with sharp edges and pointed tips. Later, the Celts crafted long slashing swords with blunted tips. These longer slashing swords could inflict more injury and may have been developed to be used by warriors on horseback, although historians are unclear on this fact. The Celts carried their swords in beautifully decorated scabbards that were covered with bronze and ironwork motifs. The Celts also used daggers in combat, and these were also carried in decorated sheaths.

Celts used spears, javelins, and lances with great skill. Some Celtic coins from Britain even depict Celtic warriors brandishing their spears in battle. Spears were an incredibly effective weapon for a Celtic warrior. A spear thrown at the beginning of a battle could maim or kill the enemy, or it might pierce an enemy's shield and stay there. This would force him to throw away his shield and open himself up for attack.

The Celtic names for many of their spears have survived to modern times, illustrating the influence of these deadly weapons. The Celtic word for their light spear, for example, was *lanciae* or *lancea*. It later became the English *lance*. Other words, according to Ellis, included "The *mataris*, from which come *matara* and *materi*, a pike, was also adopted from the Celtic. A *gaesum* was a strong heavy javelin, and the root *gae* for spear is easily recognizable in Irish. There was also a *tragula*, a light javelin."[92]

The Celts also carried superior shields that gave them a great deal of protection in battle. Their large shields were straight along the sides and rounded at each end. Some shields

THE BRONZE SHIELD OF BATTERSEA

In the mid 1800s, a strange object was dredged up from the bottom of the Thames River in England. It turned out to be a large bronze Celtic shield. Frank Delaney quotes one description of the shield in his book *The Celts*:

> Of bronze and enamel panels attached . . . by twenty four rivets [small metal objects used to attach metal] with washers. Each of the three panels has been decorated with nine roundels [round metal pieces] inlaid with red enamel. . . . The central boss [raised part of the flat surface] of the shield rises above the surrounding surface, roundel-decorated too, a gleaming centerpiece, and so lavish and delicate seems the whole work, with inlaid glass and vivid color, and abstract suggestions of fearsome facial expressions, that much speculation has focused on whether it was designed for battle at all.

Researchers believe, in fact, that the beautiful Battersea shield was never used for combat. Its location in the water suggests that it might have been an offering to the gods. Today it stands as a symbol of the independent Celtic warrior spirit.

were made of wood, but others were made of bronze. The Celts decorated their shields with swirling patterns and images of animals, such as the boar, that represented strength.

On their heads the Celts wore iron helmets. By the La Tène period, these heavy, effective helmets had replaced the weaker bronze war helmets. The Celts put fabulous decorations such as animal figures, horns, and hinged cheek pieces on their helmets. Many of these decorations may have also represented a particular god or animal that the Celts revered.

Some Celtic helmets also had a large knob that protruded from the top. This knob was purely a Celtic invention. The fact that many ancient writers commented on it indicates that it was very unusual. The helmets were so effective at protecting warriors that the knob style was almost immediately adopted by the Celts' enemies.

The Chariot

By far, however, the most effective thing that the Celts used in battle was the fast war chariot. It is not clear when the Celts first adopted the chariot, but their chariot warfare was highly developed by the time the Romans began recording it. Additionally, chariots have been found in many lavish Celtic burial sites, suggesting that they held a great importance to the Celtic people.

The Celts used a light, two-wheeled war chariot that was pulled by a pair of small horses. The body of the chariot was usually made of lightweight wickerwork or perhaps wood with bronze fittings and iron wheels. Most Celtic chariots carried two men, the charioteer and the warrior. During battle, a

battalion of chariots galloped toward the opposing army as the warriors heaved spears and javelins at their foes. Then the warriors jumped from the chariots to engage in battle, and the charioteers drove the vehicle back away from the fighting. Each driver waited at the edge of the battle and watched his particular warrior as he fought. If the tide of battle turned, or if the warrior got into trouble, the charioteer would rush back into battle and help the warrior.

The Celts were one of the few societies that continued to use chariot warfare centuries after it had fallen into disuse throughout the rest of the ancient world. They became masters of this war vehicle, and the Romans were shocked when they faced Celtic chariot armies. After facing such an army, Caesar, for example, wrote, "They have become so efficient that even on steep slopes they can control their horses at full gallop, check and turn them in a moment, run along the pole, stand on the yoke and get back to the chariot with incredible speed."[93]

The chariot was one of the things that enabled the Celts to hold their own against the onslaught of the Roman invasion in the first century A.D. By the time the Romans began to write about the Celtic civilization's advanced chariot skills, they were seasoned warriors whose daily lives were filled with battle and warfare. Celtic life revolved around military strength. They relied on warfare to increase their wealth. Warriors who achieved glory in battle were among the most respected people in Celtic society. They were savage, powerful, brave, and honorable, and they survive in the stories and legends that celebrate their achievements.

CHAPTER SEVEN

THE LONG DEFEAT

By the fourth century B.C., the Celtic civilization had spread throughout Europe and what is now Great Britain. Celtic tribes had built large settlements and farmed the land, bringing new technological innovations to the rest of the world. Their artwork rivaled, even surpassed, that of other cultures. Even so, their civilization had already begun its decline. The defeat of the Celts did not happen at once. Rather, a combination of factors over the course of centuries ensured that by the middle of the first century A.D., the Celtic civilization that had once been so magnificent would be almost completely forgotten.

A Lack of Tribal Unity

One of the civilization's greatest weaknesses was also one of its hallmarks: the independence of its tribal leaders. Each Celtic tribe was governed by an individual leader who held the power within the group. The warriors of that tribe followed their king because they respected him rather than simply because he was a commander. The king chose when and where to conduct warfare, and his warriors were bound by their loyalty to follow him and him alone. To many, it would be unthinkable to follow anyone else.

This independence created strong fighting units that were bound to one another but not to the society as a whole. There was never a central leader within the whole

Celtic civilization, or no great center of Celtic power where the best warriors could be found. Tribe fought against tribe for land, cattle, and wealth. Weaker tribes were destroyed, while stronger tribes built magnificent hill-forts called *oppidas* and traded with the rest of the world.

If an outsider threatened one tribe, the rest of the tribes did not necessarily come to its aid. Sometimes, if a threat was too large to be ignored, tribes would ally to fight a common enemy. But even then, no one could agree on one leader. In this way, invaders could defeat one small group of Celts at a time until they achieved victory. As Delaney puts it,

> The disparate Celts never could organise; their resistance to invasion and colonisation never achieved success. Their attitudinal individuality precluded nationality; they never attained the same depth of political and military unity which had enabled Rome to become a cohesive Empire. The story of the Celts' decline becomes a tale of utter colonisation, of being subsumed by other cultures, Romans, Saxons, Vikings, Normans.[94]

Outside enemies were not the only threat to the Celtic civilization. Unrest and warfare from within also contributed to the Celts' eventual downfall. Individual warring Celtic chieftains further weakened society. Since much of the Celts' wealth and stature came from raiding one another, it was inevitable that many tribes became enemies. Continued warfare and mistrust between individual chieftains threw Celtic life into a chaos of fear and unease.

The Celtic ideal of loyalty to a leader also played a role in this unease. Because warriors were bound by honor and loyalty to their leader, they were expected to follow him without question. If a leader made bad decisions or fought unfair battles, the warriors were torn between their obligation to their leader and their feelings about his actions. This sometimes resulted in feuds within a tribe as loyalties were tested. Caesar commented on this, saying, "There are factions not only in all the states, and in all the cantons and their divisions, but almost in each family, and of these factions . . . the leaders [are those] who are considered according to their judgement to possess the greatest influence."[95]

In Europe, sometime during the last century B.C., the power of the Celtic chieftains began to give way to a new form of government within the tribes. New tribal leaders, called *vergobret*, who acted somewhat like presidents, rose to power. Ancient writers such as Caesar mentioned these leaders, but little else is known about this new development in Celtic culture. Some tribes had both a king and a *vergobret*, which created conflict within the tribe.

It is not clear exactly what role the *vergobret* played in Celtic civilization. However, historians suspect that the appeareance of this new governmental figure reflects the increased Roman influence on Celtic tribes in Europe because the word (a Latin term) is of Roman origin. But in the end, even this new form of leadership could not stem the tide of conquest that was roaring toward the Celtic civilization.

The Romans Conquer the Celts

In 58 B.C., Roman commander Julius Caesar invaded Gaul with the intention of conquering and suppressing the Celtic tribes. By the time Caesar entered Gaul, the Celts were in political chaos. At the time, three powerful Celtic tribes—the Aedui, the Sequani, and the Arverni—were struggling for control of the area. Non-Celtic tribes from Germany, such as the Suevi, were pressing into Gaul from the north as Caesar's Roman army invaded from the south. The three Celtic tribes were too busy fighting one another to realize the danger.

About 71 B.C., the Suevi had invaded and defeated the Aedui. In desperation, Divitiacus, the Aedui *vergobret*, traveled to Rome to ask for help in protecting his tribe against the invading Suevi. Roman leaders agreed to help, an opportunity that gave Caesar the excuse he needed to begin his conquest. Although some of the Celtic tribes eventually banded together against him, it was a lost cause. One by one, Caesar fought the tribes until all of Gaul was defeated.

But one Celtic warrior in Gaul, Vercingetorix of the Arverni, refused defeat. He managed to unite the Celts into a huge army to oppose Caesar. His name, which means superior war king, suggests that he had incredible power among the Celtic tribes, and he became the commander-in-chief of the Celtic forces in Gaul.

For a few months between 53 and 52 B.C., Vercingetorix and his Celtic warriors

Romans Invade Britain

In the years following the defeat in Gaul, the Celtic civilization began to decline dramatically. Gaul came under Roman control, and the Celtic tribes, broken and scattered, were only a shadow of their former glory. But Gaul was not Caesar's only victory against the Celts. During Caesar's seven-year conquest (from 58 to 51 B.C.), he invaded Britain as well.

Although the Celts in Britain managed to hang on to their lands longer than the Celts of Europe, they were also crippled by internal fighting and intertribal warfare. Chadwick describes the political landscape of Celtic Britain, "The country was divided into a number of separate kingdoms, and there was no sort of political unity. . . . Some had an *oppidum*, often a great hill-top citadel where many could take refuge, but apparently there was no overall 'policy', no agreement among the tribal kingdoms on methods of warfare."[97]

The political landscape of Celtic Britain looked much the same as it had in Gaul when Caesar began his campaign. Some British Celts such as the Brigantes were intent on keeping their independence, while the Cantii, the Trinovantes, and the Iceni had already partially embraced Roman rule and were prepared to enter treaty relationships with them. Other tribes continued to fight one another in bitter struggles for power and wealth.

Caesar entered Britain for the first time in 55 B.C., but he left soon after. He returned again in 54 B.C. with a massive force of more than eight hundred ships, transporting thousands of Roman soldiers to Celtic shores. Almost immediately, many Celtic tribes forgot their personal battles and united together to face the Roman threat. One Celt, Cassivel-

A statue of Gallic leader Vercingetorix, who led a revolt against Julius Caesar's Romans In 53-52 B.C.

managed to hand Caesar a series of defeats. But it was not to last. The Celts' downfall came at the battle of Alesia, in Gaul. There, Caesar's army surrounded the Celts and besieged them. Faced with the choice of surrender or starvation, Vercingetorix decided to save the Celtic people and surrender himself to the Romans. Delaney describes what followed, "In true Celtic tradition [Vercingetorix] put on his finest robes, went forth to Caesar's tent and laid down his sword at Caesar's feet. For six years the Romans kept Vercingetorix prisoner. On Caesar's triumphant return they paraded the Celt like an exotic animal through Rome and then strangled him."[96]

launus, became leader of the entire Celtic force. Under his leadership, the Celts battled Caesar and defeated him in many battles.

However, Caesar's Roman force could not be stopped. Slowly, battle after battle, Caesar cut through the Celtic armies. Finally, it was clear that the Romans would be victorious. The Celtic resolve crumbled, and many tribal leaders sent ambassadors to Caesar asking for peace. He agreed, providing that the Celtic tribes would pay homage to Rome as the ruler of Britain. Many of them did. From that moment on, Britain was under Roman rule.

Caesar might have defeated the Celts, but he did not destroy them. Many Celtic tribes continued to fight Roman armies for years, hoping to defeat the hated conquerers and regain their lands. Time and again, Rome sent troops to quell Celtic uprisings. Except in the farthest reaches of Scotland and Ireland, the Celts were always subdued.

Effects of the Roman Occupation

Although Caesar handed the Celts a crushing defeat, they were not wiped out. Any power that individual tribes had was diminished, but many Celtic tribes continued to remain independent throughout Europe and Great Britain. Some tribes realized that Rome held all the power and decided to ally with their former enemy. Other tribes violently opposed the Roman occupation. This change had a great impact on Celtic society. In the past, tribes that fought one another knew that their success or failure in battle relied on the prowess and skill of a tribe's members. If a leader felt that his warriors could defeat the warriors from another tribe, he would attack. Now, however, Celtic chieftains who attacked a tribe that was allied with Rome had a new problem. That tribe could plead with their powerful Roman rulers for help. The old tradition of raiding

A painting of the Roman siege at Alesia. The final defeat of Vercingetorix's army here in 52 B.C. ended all hope of Celtic independence in Gaul.

"THEY MAKE A DESERT AND CALL IT PEACE"

There are many accounts of Roman victories against the Celts, but few give details from the Celtic point of view. However, one historian, named Tacitus, attempted to record the words of a Celtic leader. Tacitus documented the campaign of the Roman commander Agricola against the Scottish Celts in A.D. 80. Tacitus claims to have reported a speech given by the Celtic king Calgacus before the battle. Although it is questionable whether these words were actually spoken, the despair of the Celts was undoubtedly very real. Calgacus's words suggest that the Romans would stop at nothing until they destroyed the Celtic way of life, leaving a "desert" in which no remnants of Celtic culture would survive. Myles Dillon and Nora Chadwick in their book, *The Celtic Realms*, quote the bitter Celtic commander:

> The extremity of the earth is ours, . . . but this is the end of the habitable world. . . . The Romans are in the heart of our country. . . . No submission can satisfy their pride. . . . While the land has anything left it is the theater of war. . . . They make a desert and call it peace.

for wealth and honor was no longer possible under the continued threat of Roman alliances and attack.

Roman rulers were completely aware of Rome's effect on Celtic society. They understood that the best way to truly conquer a civilization was to change the people's way of life, and they lost no time in trying to eradicate the Celtic culture. Rome rewarded friendly Celtic kings with Roman titles, riches, land, and a taste for the so-called civilized Roman way of life. Roman clothing and titles became status symbols, and many Celts embraced their new lifestyles. Celts married Romans, and the Celtic culture was further diluted as a result.

This assimilation into the Roman ways devastated the Celtic civilization more than anything else, and the Romans knew it. The ancient writer Tacitus eloquently described the social changes that wrecked Celtic culture,

> To induce a people, prone to fight, to grow pleasurably inured to peace and ease, Agricola [a Roman commander] . . . trained the sons of the chiefs in the liberal arts and expressed a preference for British natural ability over the trained skill of the Gauls. The result was that in place of distaste for the Latin language came a passion to command it. In the same way, our national dress came into favor and the toga was everywhere to be seen. And so the Britons were gradually led on to the amenities [such as] . . . arcades,

baths, and sumptuous banquets. They spoke of such novelties as civilization when really they were only a feature of their enslavement.[98]

As the Celts embraced the Roman way of life, they abandoned their own culture and beliefs. They began to cremate their dead instead of creating the lavish burials filled with rich grave goods. The glorious original artwork that the Celts were known for began to decline. Little by little, the small details of Celtic life died out.

The Celts and Christianity

At about the same time that Caesar was successfully invading Gaul and Britain, another movement was slowly gaining hold in the world: Christianity. This new religion, which taught that there was only one God instead of many gods, began spreading through Europe during the first century A.D. By the fourth century, there were Christian communities in many areas of Gaul.

When Rome conquered Gaul, many Gauls took advantage of Roman citizenship and Roman education. By the fourth century A.D. Gaul was considered to be one of the greatest intellectual areas of Europe. Many influential thinkers of the day were Gauls. As Christianity spread, many members of the ruling and intellectual classes embraced this new faith. These men became the leaders and rulers of many communities in Gaul, and they influenced many other Gauls. Christianity was seen as a positive force in society.

As Christianity grew in power, religious leaders in Gaul put pressure on local groups to desert their pagan faith in the old gods. Temples were destroyed, and churches were built in their places. People no longer gave offerings to their gods by casting objects into sacred rivers and streams. Sculptures and other artworks that depicted the pagan gods were deliberately destroyed. Anyone who worshipped Celtic gods was stripped of civil rights. Slowly, the old ways were abandoned.

Things were somewhat different in Britain and Ireland. Although Caesar had defeated many Celtic tribes in Britain during his invasion, he did not penetrate too far into the country itself. In many rural areas, Rome had little influence on daily life, so people continued to worship the Celtic gods and follow their traditional ways of life.

An early christian cross. During the 4th and 5th centuries, Christianity spread throughout Celtic society.

In the larger British towns, however, the Romans encouraged aristocratic Celts to adopt the Roman way of life, although they still allowed the native religions to continue alongside the Roman beliefs. In this way, Celtic culture was not eradicated in the same way it had been in Europe.

It is unknown exactly when Christianity came to Britain, but historians believe it might have been about the same time that it rose to prominence in Gaul. Regardless, by the fifth century A.D. Christianity was firmly established. Ireland, too, had converted to Christianity by this time, and it was due in large part to the work of one man, St. Patrick.

St. Patrick Comes to Ireland

Details about Patrick's early life are scanty. He was born in Britain in the late 300s A.D., and some historians suspect he was half Roman, half Celtic. When he was sixteen years old, his village was attacked by Irish Celts, and the boy was sold into slavery. For six years, he lived among his Celtic captors until he managed to escape and make his way back to his family in Britain. Eventually, he entered the Christian priesthood and, at some point, decided to become a missionary to Ireland.

Historians suspect that Christianity had already been introduced in Ireland before Patrick's arrival, but he was certainly influential in spreading it throughout the country. He spoke a Celtic language and was very familiar with the tribal systems and way of life. The Celts, he knew, revered their leaders. Kings were the center of the spiritual beliefs of a tribe. As historian Delaney explains,

So dependent was the society upon the family, the kinship structure, that

the king had more than temporal [superficial] influence—he possessed sacred connotations, influenced the spirituality and morality of his tribe with his power to officiate at worship, with his central role in all religious expression and with his court of warriors, jurists, and Druids.[99]

Patrick used this knowledge to his advantage and was incredibly successful. Many Celtic kings converted to Christianity, and, as Patrick predicted, so did their tribes. By the time of Patrick's death in A.D. 493, Christianity was firmly established in Ireland, and the old ways of life were dying.

A lithograph depicts St. Patrick in Ireland. Patrick used his knowledge of Celtic culture to convert many Celtic kings to Christianity.

Effects of Christianity

Christianity created profound changes in the Celtic civilization of Britain and Ireland. When the beliefs of the Christian church supplanted Celtic religious beliefs, they also affected the people's way of life. Every part of Celtic life that revolved around the worship of their deities—the inauguration of kings, the strength of their warriors, the cunning of their druids—was removed. Christian religious leaders preached that the pagan Celtic gods that were once part of daily life were now demons to be feared. The monasteries, not the kings, became the centers of religious worship.

But it wasn't easy to discard the old ways. Many Celts resisted the new religion and continued to worship their own gods, especially in rural areas where the local culture had more influence. In response, Christian leaders gave Christian saints names and powers similar to the existing Celtic gods and goddesses. Slowly, the old deities decreased in power as the new Christian ones took their places. As Ross explains, "Christianity eventually displaced the old religion, but many of the pagan gods and goddesses are still traceable in the characters of local saints, and the spirits of individual localities."[100]

One example of this change is the Celtic goddess Brigit [Brigid in Christianity]. She was one of the most powerful mother-goddesses of Celtic religion; the Celtic celebration of one of their most important holidays, Imbolc, included prayers and worship to this goddess every February 1. After Christianity, Brigit became St. Brigid, and Catholic Christians still celebrate her feast day on February 1. The transformation of Brigit/Brigid is one example of how the Christian church adopted Celtic beliefs and changed them to reflect the new beliefs.

Christianity Changes the Druids

Christianity also had a profound and complex effect on the Celtic druids. In the Celtic belief, knowledge was kept secret, and the power of knowledge was kept with the druids, who studied and understood the ancient learning. They believed that nothing should ever be written down in their own language, so they never left any written records behind. Their silence and intelligence created an air of mystery around them. However, the Christian monks changed that. The Christian faith revolves around the Bible, which is considered the written word of God. Monks and religious leaders were expected to be able to read and write and to record information. The arrival of literacy destroyed the druids' power of silence. No longer could they claim to hold all knowledge, when knowledge was written down to be read.

On the other hand, Christianity released the druids from their cage of silence, enabling them to record their own histories for the first time. The early Christian church in Ireland was the seat of learning and knowledge for society, and the druids, naturally wanted to be a part of it. Many former druids embraced Christianity as a result, and they set about recording their knowledge. In Christianity, say Dillon and Chadwick, "The Celtic genius found its fullest expression and realized its greatest achievement. . . . By the sixth century Irish Christianity surpassed that of every other land in western Europe, not only in intensity and sanctity, but also in passionate devotion to learning."[101]

ST. PATRICK AND THE SNAKES

When St. Patrick arrived in Ireland, his goal was to convert pagan civilization, which worshipped many gods, to Christianity. His efforts resulted in Christianity replacing much of the traditional Celtic religion. Along the way, many myths sprang up about the legendary powers of St. Patrick.

The best-known legend involves Patrick driving the snakes from Ireland. Various stories recount that Patrick stood on a hill and used a wooden staff to drive the serpents into the sea, banishing them forever from the land. Although it is true that there are no snakes in Ireland, some speculate that St. Patrick's driving the snakes was a metaphor for his success in driving the Celtic pagan religions from Ireland.

Much of the Celtic mythology, legend, and history then was written down in the early centuries of Christianity. Monks painstakingly hand-lettered hundreds of pages, filled with the stories from their Celtic history and recording heroes, gods, and legends for the first time. They also decorated the pages of their manuscripts and bibles with extraordinary artwork in the style of the great swirling forms and designs of the La Tène period.

By the ninth century A.D., Christianity had pervaded most of Celtic Britain and Ireland. Established monasteries were a regular feature in many villages. However, other areas of Britain and Ireland were still under Celtic control. In these places, there was still no organized form of government, and local chieftains held the most power. Because these villages were located so far north, they were insulated from invasion and conquest that befell other parts of Europe during that time. But all of that changed with the appearance of the Vikings.

Viking Invasions and Their Effect

In 789 A.D., the Vikings seemed to come out of nowhere to ravage Ireland, the last seat of Celtic civilization and the center of learning for the Celtic culture at the time. They set out from the Scandinavian countries, particularly Norway, and traveled on boats carved like dragons. The Vikings' goal was to acquire wealth. At first, they attacked and destroyed the monasteries along the costal areas of Ireland. Then they turned their attention inland, and soon the entire country lived in fear of the deadly Viking attacks.

The raids continued throughout the ninth and tenth centuries. The Vikings overtook small Celtic seacoast villages and turned them into large seaports. By 841, the Irish areas of Wicklow, Waterford, Wexford, and Cork were Viking seaports. Each port was the center of a large, independent Viking kingdom with its own leaders, very similar to the Celtic form of independent tribal leadership. Eventually they made Dublin a chief Viking center and used it as a base for their fleet of swift dragon boats.

For two hundred years, the Celts and the Vikings lived side by side in Ireland, although the Celts continued to battle for control from the Vikings throughout that time. Finally, in 1014, the Irish won a great victory over the Vikings at the Battle of Clontarf. This put an end to Viking rule, but by that time it made little difference. Over the years, the two cultures had begun to merge. Celts and Vikings had married one another and lived together in villages throughout Ireland. Vikings had converted to Christianity, and the old Celtic ways were but a distant memory.

The Vikings' Effect

The Vikings' effect on Celtic civilization was twofold. First, they effectively wiped out most of the intellectual achievements the Irish Celts made after the Roman conquest. As Chadwick explains,

> The intellectual loss to Ireland caused by the Viking regime was enormous. Treasure, including illuminated manuscripts, liturgical vessels and reliquaries [objects used during worship], were lost, and the techniques which had inspired them were scattered. The monastic houses, the homes of all such fine work, were destroyed.[102]

The second effect of the Viking invasions was to destroy the last remnants of Celtic agricultural society. Until the first Viking raids destroyed Irish Celtic monasteries, the Celts still lived as they always had: in small villages surrounded by farmland. There were few large

towns, and Celtic lords still held power in most areas. The Vikings, however, managed to destroy the Celtic economy and way of life by altering how the local people lived and traded their goods. Viking raids forced many small communities to band together for protection, and these communites grew into towns. For the first time in Celtic history, large towns became the center of commerce and culture. Chadwick says, "Parts of Ireland . . . were so overwhelmed by the Vikings as to be transformed from a cattle-keeping country, with an exclusively internal economy, to one

The Vikings,(shown here in their long ships), arrived in Ireland in the 8th century A.D. *and in less than 300 years, wiped out the last remnants of Celtic society.*

THE BOOK OF KELLS

When the Irish Celts embraced Christianity, many of them became priests and monks in monasteries that sprang up in the Irish countryside. They spent much of their time painstakingly creating Bibles and other religious books. One of the books they made was the *Book of Kells*. No other Celtic artifact existing today can match the breathtaking beauty of this marvelous book.

The small book, measuring only about thirteen by nine and one-half inches, is a masterpiece of Celtic art. The pages resonate with complex patterns of scrollwork and ornamentation in the high La Tène Celtic style: spirals, interlocked and intertwined flourishes and designs, all unique but together creating one gorgeous image in a chaos of movement.

The Celtic love of the natural world also shines through. Small human figures, for example, hide among the swirling patterns. On one page, two cats quietly watch two rats chewing on a wafer. The book is also filled with delightful images of ordinary animals such as goats, mice, cats, and an otter catching a fish. These everyday details are, says Nora Chadwick in *The Celts*, "a reminder that the lives of small creatures and domestic animals were going on while the great events of the world were pending. . . .They remind us that the *Book of Kells* is not merely a collection of masterpieces but is also a miniature of the Celtic world of about A.D. 800."

in which the coastal areas now boasted towns, trade, and the units of measure which invariably accompany them."[103]

By the tenth century A.D., the last remnants of the Celtic civilization were gone. A few fragments remained hidden away in monasteries, where some of the books of their legends had survived. There were still places where the old gods were worshipped, but they were only shadows of their former power. In Ireland and Scotland, the clans and families held on to some influence, but they would never achieve the greatness that was once the Celtic civilization.

THE CELTS DID NOT DISAPPEAR ENTIRELY

On the surface, life remained the same for many Celts throughout the years of conquest and struggle. Daily life went on as it always had. There was no indication that things had changed.

But the world had changed. Slowly, as older people died, their memories and traditions disappeared. The Celtic culture mixed with Roman and Viking ways, adopted Christianity, and gradually assimilated into society.

There were a few pockets where the old ways remained. In the Scottish Highlands, for example, proud clans continued to be powerful. They maintained many of the old beliefs and were able to cling to their way of life because they were insulated from the rest of the world by the remoteness of their location. Great Scottish families lived, fought, and died in much the same way that their Celtic ancestors had done many centuries before. They remained basically unchanged until the 1700s, when the last of the Scottish clans were shattered by the English in the Battle of Culloden in 1746. In many ways, the defeat of the Scottish clans at Culloden mirrored the defeat of the Celtic civilization. Delaney says,

The battle of Culloden resembled in many ways a traditional engagement between Celts and Romans. The forces of the English, under the Duke of Cumberland, were arrayed neatly and in disciplined ranks. The Scots set themselves out along tribal lines, and so individual were the personalities of the clans that no clear leader could emerge to give orders. The battle went as decisively against the last Celts of Scotland as it had against Vercingetorix [in Gaul] and Boudicca [in Britain] sixteen centuries before.[104]

In Ireland, as in Scotland, the old ways lingered in the more remote areas of the country. The stories and legends of the Celts were still told. The old gods still appeared in folklore as fairies and leprechauns. Musicians and poets learned the old songs and passed them down for generations. The Irish language adapted some changes, but it remained mainly a Celtic tongue.

The most notable example of the Celts maintaining their culture is in Ireland where learning and art survived despite the invasions and conquerers of the Celtic era. Celtic art flourished under Christianity. Stone carvers created magnificent stone crosses adorned with Celtic swirls and knotwork. The stories and legends of the Celtic people were recorded for all time.

Over the centuries, other invaders tried to crush the Celtic way of life in Ireland, Scotland, and Wales. Whenever the Celts were threatened with the loss of their culture, however, a new spirit of revival took hold. The descendants of the proud Celts stubbornly refused to let go of their culture completely. Bards and court poets continued to entertain the English kings with tales of their Celtic past. Traditional music and the instruments that played it remained. The people continued to speak their language at home, even though they spoke English in public.

As a result, the Celtic civilization never died out completely, although it was no longer the powerful culture it once had been. Today, more than two million people still speak a Celtic language, and in the last few years, there has been yet another revival of the Celtic spirit in music and dance. Movies, television shows, and Broadway productions have reached into the Celtic past for inspiration. Traditional songs and instruments are once again popular.

The themes that ran through Celtic civilization were simple: love of nature, respect for one another, loyalty to a leader, and honor for everyone. These attributes can still be glimpsed in the music, stories, and art of the once-great Celtic civilization.

Notes

Chapter 1: The First Europeans

1. Peter Berresford Ellis, *Celt and Roman*. London: Constable and Company Limited, 1998, p. 3.
2. David Willis McCullough, ed., *Chronicles of the Barbarians*. New York: Random House, 1998, p. xv.
3. Barry Cunliffe, *The Celtic World*. New York: McGraw-Hill, 1979, p. 8.
4. Myles Dillon and Nora Chadwick, *The Celtic Realms*. London: Weidenfeld and Nicolson, 1967, p. 1.
5. Quoted in McCullough, *Chronicles of the Barbarians*, p. 73.
6. Quoted in McCullough, *Chronicles of the Barbarians*, p. 57.
7. T. G. E. Powell, *The Celts*. New York: Frederick A. Praeger, 1958, pp. 16–17.
8. Ellis, *Celt and Roman*, p. 17.
9. Nora Chadwick, *The Celts*. New York: Penguin Books, 1971, p. 25.
10. Ellis, *Celt and Roman*, p. 17.
11. Ellis, *Celt and Roman*, p. 19.
12. Anne Ross, *Everyday Life of the Pagan Celts*. London: B. T. Batsford Ltd., 1970, p. 21.
13. Ellis, *Celt and Roman*, p. 18.
14. Ross, *Everyday Life of the Pagan Celts*, p. 20.
15. Ross, *Everyday Life of the Pagan Celts*, p. 20.
16. Cunliffe, *The Celtic World*, p. 16.
17. Ellis, *Celt and Roman*, p. 85.

Chapter 2: Tribes and Chieftains

18. Chadwick, *The Celts*, pp. 130–31.
19. Ellis, *Celt and Roman*, p. 38.
20. Ellis, *Celt and Roman*, p. 36.
21. Ellis, *Celt and Roman*, p. 36.
22. Chadwick, *The Celts*, pp. 64–65.
23. Chadwick, *The Celts*, p. 61.
24. Powell, *The Celts*, p. 75.
25. Chadwick, *The Celts*, p. 116.
26. Ross, *Everyday Life of the Pagan Celts*, p. 119.
27. Ross, *Everyday Life of the Pagan Celts*, p. 120.
28. Dillon and Chadwick, *The Celtic Realms*, p. 88.
29. Quoted in Dillon and Chadwick, *The Celtic Realms*, p. 88.
30. Powell, *The Celts*, p. 121.
31. Quoted in Ross, *Everyday Life of the Pagan Celts*, p. 122.
32. Peter Berresford Ellis, *The Ancient World of the Celts*. London: Constable and Company Limited, 1998, p. 39.
33. Quoted in Ross, *Everyday Life of the Pagan Celts*, p. 122.

Chapter 3: Masters of Science and Technology

34. Ellis, *The Ancient World of the Celts*, p. 23.

35. Françoise Andouze and Olivier Buchsenschutz, *Towns, Villages and Countryside of Celtic Europe*. London: B. T. Batsford Ltd., 1992, p. 169.

36. Andouze and Buchsenschutz, *Towns, Villages*, p. 170.

37. Ellis, *The Ancient World of the Celts*, p. 148.

38. Quoted in McCullough, *Chronicles of the Barbarians*, p. 73.

39. Quoted in Ellis, *The Ancient World of the Celts*, p. 101.

40. Ellis, *The Ancient World of the Celts*, p. 101.

41. Ellis, *The Ancient World of the Celts*, p. 102.

42. Quoted in Ellis, *The Ancient World of the Celts*, p. 102.

43. Powell, *The Celts*, p. 90.

44. Andouze and Buchsenschutz, *Towns, Villages*, p. 162.

45. Chadwick, *The Celts*, p. 141.

46. Ellis, *The Ancient World of the Celts*, p. 107.

47. Ellis, *Celt and Roman*, p. 33.

48. Ellis, *Celt and Roman*, p. 31.

49. Andouze and Buchsenschutz, *Towns, Villages*, p. 155.

50. Ellis, *The Ancient World of the Celts*, p. 111.

51. Ellis, *The Ancient World of the Celts*, p. 112.

52. Quoted in Ellis, *The Ancient World of the Celts*, p. 121.

53. Andouze and Buchsenschutz, *Towns, Villages*, p. 85.

54. Ellis, *The Ancient World of the Celts*, p. 164.

Chapter 4: Religion, Myth, and the Druids

55. Miranda Green, *The Gods of the Celts*. Totowa, NJ: Barnes and Noble Books, 1986, p. 22.

56. Green, *The Gods of the Celts*, p. 170.

57. Frank Delaney, *The Celts*. Boston: Little, Brown and Company, 1986, p. 85.

58. Ellis, *The Ancient World of the Celts*, p. 112.

59. Green, *The Gods of the Celts*, p. 151.

60. Ross, *Everyday Life of the Pagan Celts*, p. 38.

61. Ross, *Everyday Life of the Pagan Celts*, p. 133.

62. Green, *The Gods of the Celts*, p. 72.

63. Peter Berresford Ellis, *The Druids*. Grand Rapids, MI: William B. Eerdmans Publishing Company, 1994, p. 125.

64. Green, *The Gods of the Celts*, p. 32.

65. Ross, *Everyday Life of the Pagan Celts*, p. 141.

66. Christiane Eluere, *The Celts: Conquerors of Ancient Europe*. New York: Harry Abrams Publishing, 1992, pp. 156–57.

67. Quoted in Eluere, *The Celts*, p. 159.

68. Quoted in Ellis, *The Druids*, p. 145.

Chapter 5: The Golden Age of Celtic Art

69. Dillon and Chadwick, *The Celtic Realms*, p. 278.
70. Dillon and Chadwick, *The Celtic Realms*, p. 279.
71. Ross, *Everyday Life of the Pagan Celts*, pp. 175–76.
72. Delaney, *The Celts*, p. 130.
73. Delaney, *The Celts*, p. 132.
74. Dillon and Chadwick, *The Celtic Realms*, p. 281.
75. Delaney, *The Celts*, pp. 132–33.
76. Chadwick, *The Celts*, p. 226.
77. Dillon and Chadwick, *The Celtic Realms*, pp. 283–84.
78. Ross, *Everyday Life of the Pagan Celts*, p. 181.
79. Chadwick, *The Celts*, p. 232.
80. Dillon and Chadwick, *The Celtic Realms*, p. 289.
81. Ross, *Everyday Life of the Pagan Celts*, p. 176.
82. Ross, *Everyday Life of the Pagan Celts*, p. 205.
83. Ross, *Everyday Life of the Pagan Celts*, p. 182.

Chapter 6: Warfare and Blood

84. Quoted in Ross, *Everyday Life of the Pagan Celts*, p. 56.
85. Ross, *Everyday Life of the Pagan Celts*, p. 56.
86. Quoted in Ross, *Everyday Life of the Pagan Celts*, p. 56.

87. Quoted in McCullough, *Chronicles of the Barbarians*, p. 54.
88. Quoted in Ellis, *The Ancient World of the Celts*, p. 80.
89. Ellis, *The Ancient World of the Celts*, p. 80.
90. Quoted in Ellis, *Celt and Roman*, p. 89.
91. Quoted in Ross, *Everyday Life of the Pagan Celts*, p. 67.
92. Ellis, *The Ancient World of the Celts*, p. 75.
93. Quoted in Ellis, *Celt and Roman*, p. 88.

Chapter 7: The Long Defeat

94. Delaney, *The Celts*, p. 38.
95. Quoted in McCullough, *Chronicles of the Barbarians*, p. 51.
96. Delaney, *The Celts*, p. 36.
97. Chadwick, *The Celts*, p. 68.
98. Quoted in Barry Cunliffe, *Iron Age Communities in Britain*. London: Routledge, 1991, p. 547.
99. Delaney, *The Celts*, p. 50.
100. Anne Ross, *Pagan Celtic Britain*. London: Routledge and Kegan Paul Limited, 1967, p. 233.
101. Dillon and Chadwick, *The Celtic Realms*, p. 314.
102. Chadwick, *The Celts*, p. 110.
103. Chadwick, *The Celts*, p. 105.

Epilogue: The Celts Did Not Disappear Entirely

104. Delaney, *The Celts*, p. 57.

FOR FURTHER READING

Will Fowler, *Ancient Weapons and Warfare*. New York: Lorenz Books, 1999. This thorough study of ancient weapons includes discussions about armor, shields, helmets, and weapons.

Tudor Humphries, *Eyewitness Classics: King Arthur*. New York: DK Publishing, 1998. The history and myths surrounding the legend of King Arthur are discussed.

Haze Mary Martell, *The Celts*. New York: Viking Children's Books, 1996. The question-and-answer format of this book makes learning about the Celts easy and fun.

Anne Ross and Roger Garland, *Druids, Gods and Heros from Celtic Mythology*. New York: Peter Bendick Books, 1994. One of the leading Celtic scholars, Ross gives a detailed, yet interesting, survey of Celtic myth and legend.

Major Works
Consulted

Books

Françoise Andouze and Olivier Buschsenschultz, *Towns, Villages and Countryside of Celtic Europe*. London: B. T. Batsford Ltd., 1992. This scholarly book is filled with information about Celtic life, based on archaeological finds.

D. A. Binchy, *Celtic and Anglo-Saxon Kingship*. London: Oxford Press, 1970. This book, part of a series of scholarly lectures at the University of Oxford, discusses the rituals and traditions of Celtic Kingship.

Nora Chadwick, *Celtic Britain*. New York: Frederick A. Praeger, 1963. Chadwick, a prominent Celtic scholar, gives an exhaustive survey of the Celtic civilization.

————, *The Celts*. New York: Penguin Books, 1971. Chadwick's account of Celtic history is the benchmark of Celtic scholarship.

T. C. Champion and J. V. S. Megaw, eds., *Settlement and Society: Aspects of West European Prehistory in the First Millennium* B.C. New York: St Martin's Press, 1985. Champion and Megaw have edited a dense, scholarly book of essays written by prominent Celtic and Iron Age historians.

Grahame Clark, *Prehistoric Britain*. London: B. T. Batsford Ltd., 1962. This dense book focuses on the Iron Age era of Great Britain.

Barry Cunliffe, *The Celtic World*. New York: McGraw-Hill, 1979. This large coffee-table book is a beautifully illustrated guide to the history of the Celts.

————, *Iron Age Communities in Britain*. London: Routledge, 1991. A thick, densely packed tome focusing on early Iron Age archaeology.

Frank Delaney, *The Celts*. Boston: Little, Brown and Company, 1986. This easy-to-read book is a complete overview of Celtic history, with nice photos.

Myles Dillon and Nora Chadwick, *The Celtic Realms*. London: Weidenfeld and Nicholson, 1967. These two distinguished historians have written a comprehensive overview of the history of the Celtic civilization.

Peter Berresford Ellis, *The Ancient World of the Celts*. London: Constable and Company Limited, 1998. Ellis, a respected Celtic historian, gives a complete overview of the history of the Celtic civilization.

————, *Celt and Roman*. London: Constable and Company Limited, 1998. This book is a lively and interesting account of the clashes between Celts and Romans.

————, *The Druids*, Grand Rapids, MI: William B. Eerdmans Publishing Company, 1994. Although little concrete evidence of the druids exists, Ellis has managed to write a fact-filled book on the history and culture of the Celtic druids.

Christine Eluere, *The Celts: Conquerors of Ancient Europe*. New York: Harry Abrams Publishing, 1992. An easy-to-read, beautifully illustrated short history of the Celts.

Stephen S. Evans, *The Lords of Battle*. Suffolk, England: Boydell & Brewer Ltd., 1997. This scholarly book focuses on battle and the importance of warfare to Celtic society.

Miranda Green, *The Gods of the Celts*. Totowa, NJ: Barnes and Noble Books, 1986. This overview of Celtic deities and beliefs covers every aspect of the Celtic religious system.

Magdolna Hellebrandt, *Celtic Finds from Northern Hungary*. Budapest, Hungary: Alademiai Kiado, 1999. An account and field notes of an archaeological dig in Europe, this book also includes many line drawings of Celtic artifacts.

Benjamin Hudson and Vickie Ziegler, *Crossed Paths: Methodological Approaches to the Celtic Aspect of the European Middle Ages*. Lanham, MD: University of America Press, 1991. This small, dense book is a scholarly account of Celtic life.

Proinsias MacCana, *Celtic Mythology*. London: Hamlyn Publishing Group, 1970. This is a good general overview book of the Celtic religion, with an emphasis on archaeology.

David Willis McCullough, ed., *Chronicles of the Barbarians*. New York: Random House, 1998. Eyewitness accounts of warfare and invasions—

including Celtic battles with the Romans—make this a lively, interesting read.

E. R. Norman, *The Early Development of Irish Society*. London: Cambridge University Press, 1969. Norman studies the history of Celtic homes, fields, and hill-forts through aerial photography.

T. G. E. Powell, *The Celts*. New York: Frederick A. Praeger, 1958. This account of Celtic history includes a great deal of information about the daily lives of the ancient Celts.

Anne Ross, *Everyday Life of the Pagan Celts*. London: B. T. Batsford Ltd., 1970. This is a detailed account of the life and society of the Celts.

———, *Pagan Celtic Britain*. London: Routledge and Kegan Paul Limited, 1967. An exhaustive account of the lives and beliefs of the Celts in Britain.

Periodicals

"Celtic Surgeon," *Discover*, March 1998.

John Collins, "Celtic Myths," *Antiquity*, March 1997.

Dora Jane Hamblin, "Once Maligned, Celts Are Now Touted as the First Europeans," *Smithsonian*, May 1993.

Robert Wernick, "What Were the Druids Like, and Was Lindow Man One?" *Smithsonian*, March 1988.

INDEX

PICTURE CREDITS

ABOUT THE AUTHOR

Award-winning children's magazine editor and writer Allison Lassieur has published more than two dozen books about history, world cultures, and health. A writer for magazines such as *National Geographic World*, *Highlights for Children*, *Scholastic News*, and *Disney Adventures*, she also writes novels, puzzle books, and computer game materials. In addition to writing, Ms. Lassieur studies medieval history. She lives and works in Pennsylvania